Don't Mind Him; He's Pregnant

DON'T MIND HIM; HE'S PREGNANT

The Man's Side of the Story

BY MARK HALLEN

Ten Speed Press

Quotations from the following works
are used with the permissions of the publishers.

Husband-Coached Childbirth by Robert A. Bradley. © 1965.
Harper & Row.

Constructive Playthings Catalog. © 1986.

Recipe for Healthy Babies. © 1979. March of Dimes.

Excerpts reprinted from "Parents Talk about Labor,"
"Sing to Your Baby," and "Welcome to Parenthood,"
Expecting Magazine, © 1986 by Gruner & Jahr USA Publishing.

Excerpts from *Pre-Parent Advisor*, © New Parent Series,
reprinted with the permission of the publisher,
Whittle Communications, Knoxville, Tennessee.

1⊛

TEN SPEED PRESS
P.O. Box 7123
Berkeley, California 94707

Book Design by Nancy Austin
Cover Design by Brent Beck

Library of Congress Cataloging-in-Publication Data

Hallen, Mark, 1954–
Don't mind him, he's pregnant.

1. Pregnancy. 2. Fathers. 3. Pregnant women—
Family relationships. I. Title. [DNLM: 1. Family—
popular works. 2. Fathers—popular works. 3. Pregnancy—
popular works. WQ 150 H184d]
RG525.H245 1987   618.2   86–23114
ISBN 0–89815–196–1

Printed in the United States of America

1 2 3 4 5 — 91 90 89 88 87

To Barbara and Casey,
without whom
I never would have experienced
the joys of fatherhood.

CONTENTS

vii

5. THE SECOND TRIMESTER / 38
or "Are We Going Camping? Uh, Sorry, Nice Blouse, Dear."

6. THE THIRD TRIMESTER / 54
or "You Want Rhythm? Get Ringo Starr in the Delivery Room With You!"

7. THE BIRTH / 120
or "Okay, Okay! You Don't Want to Breathe, You Don't Have to Breathe.

8. OUR FIRST DAYS AS A FAMILY / 131
or "Forget Every Baby You've Ever Seen—Ours Is the Most Beautiful, Cutest, Best Baby That's Ever Been Swaddled. Don't Even Think That You Have Even the Remotest Chance of Having a Baby That Can Even Come Close."

Chapter 1

MAKING THE DECISION

OR

"What Do You Mean You're Not Putting Your Thing In?"

The Biological Clock (and Why It Doesn't Have a Snooze Alarm)

It wasn't my idea. I would have been perfectly content as half of a happy yuppie couple, quietly acquiring things and asking people to give us the names of their financial consultants.

My wife, Barbara, however, had been asking people for the names of their OBGYNs. She had different ideas. Illogical ideas.

Dumb ideas.

Like the idiot teenager in a B horror movie, she had been swallowed whole by a gushing, oozing, jellied monster. The movie could have been called *The Maternal Instinct That Ate Tokyo.*

At the start of our story, I was a thirty-one-year-old co–creative director of an ad agency that specializes in direct response advertising. They'd kill me for saying this, but what I actually did was supervise the creation of junk mail (although, if I do say so myself, it was a hell of a lot better than the average junk mail; it was, in fact, very good, even excellent, junk mail) and those long TV commercials with the toll-free phone numbers.

Well, somebody has to do it.

My wife was a thirty-one-year-old freelance art director, specializing in, um, direct response advertising. Yes, it's a junk mail marrage.

Barbara is beautiful, cute, talented, and loving, and I can't think of anyone I'd rather spend my life with. True, she doesn't play word games very well, but I consider this a minor shortcoming given all her other attributes.

The two of us live and work on the island of Manhattan because we particularly enjoy subways, ridiculously high real estate costs, and Tofutti on every block.

My story begins about two years ago. Barb and I had been married two blissful years, and were in bed reading late one night when the alarm rang. It was a nasty sort of ring, very persistent, insistently grating:

"Baaaaaaaabeeeeeeeeeeeeeee!"

I jumped from our platform bed and searched for intruders. There was silence except for the gurgle of the humidifier and the generic orchestration of traffic on Sixth Avenue. A teenager yelled for somebody named "Skeech." The old lady downstairs was playing Johnny Carson for the whole neighborhood.

I began to get back into bed, but then I heard it again: "Baaaaaaaabeeeeeeeeeeeeeee!"

Barbara was sitting up now, her eyes glowing demonically in the dark. She began speaking in tongues, uttering phrases I could not comprehend:

"I want a baaaaaaaabeeeeeeeee!"

Her voice had become lower and had turned gravelly. She sounded something like Orson Welles. Her hair stood on end. The bed shuddered and lifted off the floor, depositing drawersful of underwear on the carpeting.

"Your mother had one!" she screamed, and then green stuff came flowing out of her mouth like mint chip Häagen Dazs.

Her head turned 360 degrees and the bed fell to the floor

with a bang. Finally there was only the sound of the Levelors rattling in the wind, which came through windows I didn't remember having opened.

Barbara was turning on the bedlight. "It shouldn't come as such a shock to you," she said in her normal voice. "I told you I was going to want one when we got married."

I giggled uneasily. "I thought you were kidding."

She wasn't. "I wasn't," she said.

"But it's only been two years," I protested. "I thought it would be longer. A decade or two at least."

She wasn't laughing. "I'm running out of time."

I understood this as a reference to the biological clock, a chronograph so exacting it puts the Swiss to shame. This precision timepiece had been ticking constantly since we had moved in together; it seemed to need no winding or battery and was disgustingly dependable.

"When we go away in February, I'm going to leave my thing at home," she announced.

We were going to Puerto Rico in February, one month hence.

"Then I'll leave *my* thing at home," I replied. It would be good to travel light.

Barbara smiled. "Oh, come on, you'll make a terrific father." This prediction was accompanied by a soothing caress, as if to say, "Don't worry, everything will be fine, even though . . .

. . . YOU HATE KIDS!"

Okay, maybe *hate* is too strong a word. I thought of kids the way I thought of brussels sprouts: If *you* like 'em, fine, but keep 'em away from me.

You may ask how I could dislike cute little innocent babies. For one thing, I never had the opportunity to get used to them since I was an only child. The only baby I ever had to be around was me. And the way my parents described my babyhood, it didn't sound like anything I wanted to be part of.

More important I was carrying a curse. I remember that when I was growing up my mother would often put her hands on her hips and say something like, "I hope your children eat your heart out like you eat mine." How could I subject my lovely wife to the heart-eating child my mother had willed upon me?

It was logical that I would not like kids: We have nothing in common. I like organization; kids are anarchists. I'm very competitive; kids are too easy to beat in any game I like to play. I like to tell jokes; babies do not get the punch lines. I have a short attention span; kids keep wanting to play long after the two minutes I've allotted are up.

And those were just concerns I had about other people's babies. The thought of a baby I could call my own—a living, breathing, inescapable dependent—was something only Stephen King could dream up.

My mind was wrought with fearful questions:

1. Could we afford a baby *and* a video club membership?

2. Where would we put the baby in our one-bedroom apartment and, more important, who would give up closet space to store baby things?

3. Would a baby drastically change our life-style of being able to go out at ten o'clock to a big party at some club, or take off to the Hamptons on a moment's notice, or fly to the Coast on a whim? (We never actually did any of these things, but we liked knowing we could if we wanted to.)

4. Would I like a baby if it was mine, and if not, would I be able to get enough for it on the black market to pay for a time-share in the Caribbean?

As you might expect, space and money were the biggest fears. At what point would we need a bigger place and would we have enough money for it, given what it costs to have a baby, raise it, put it in schools, send it to the movies, and buy it a computer?

Barbara chose to ignore all these concerns as she attempted to synchronize her clock to my watch. And as she stored her diaphragm in the closet with our tax records, she left no doubt about what time it was. It was, unarguably, time to have a baby.

Knocking Up Is Hard to Do

As the suitcases filled up for the Puerto Rico trip, and the diaphragm went in a box labeled "Canceled checks, 1983," I searched for a way out of my predicament.

I was not completely without hope. There was a fellow at the office who was always lamenting about how he and his wife could not bear children. There was that possibility. Then there was the wisdom I had come across in seventh grade, from a sage named Kevin Kilowitz, who preached that excess masturbation (what a seventh grader means by *excess* masturbation is anybody's guess) used up all your sperm so you wouldn't have any later when you wanted it. I didn't know whatever happened to Kevin, but I hoped he was right and that my hand had been busy enough when I was a teenager.

Finally, under the assumption that Kevin was wrong (he did, after all, take shop classes), I was planning an extensive training program in the backstroke for sperm.

Of course I also had my wits. Maybe a surrogate would work. I suggested a puppy. A parrot. A spider monkey.

At least that seemed to warrant a reply. "Spider monkeys are vicious," she said.

"No they're not," I argued. "They're cute. You can dress them up and if they turn out bad, you can sell them to a laboratory."

I gave up on this tactic when even the promise of a mink coat did not budge the diaphragm from the storage closet.

We returned from Puerto Rico with five T-shirts, three bottles of rum, and two souvenir piña colada glasses, but no baby. This last, of course, we didn't know about until some two weeks later, when Barbara announced the arrival of her period as if informing me that Richard Nixon was trying to get into our co-op. It was the start of a new monthly ritual; three days of constant sex, two weeks of waiting, then the bad news.

It wasn't that terrible, except when one of the three days came on a poker night: "Sorry, guys, can't play tonight; my wife's fertile."

After three months, Barbara sought help. The doctor apparently used phrases such as "at your age," and Barb was beginning to think that maybe her clock was running a little late after all.

The doctor gave her a diary and a thermometer. As I understood it, a woman's body temperature naturally rises and falls in a cycle every month, so if you keep track of it, you'll know precisely when you're fertile. Personally I had never doubted Barbara's accuracy in regard to her fertility, but modern medicine was out to pinpoint it with the utmost precision.

Barbara was to take her temperature every day and record her findings in the diary. This would yield a graph similar to those you see in a newspaper's financial section. Barbara studied this graph long and hard every day, until there was a dip followed by an upsurge. This indicated, I came to realize, a bull market.

Now I have to admit I wasn't totally supportive of this whole temperature idea. For one thing this graph charted minute changes, literally fractions of a degree. What if, I asked Barbara, she happened to be slightly ill one morning, just enough to nudge the mercury up a smidge? She patiently explained that she was looking for overall trends and that a one-

or two-day aberration wouldn't matter much. She was start-ing to sound alarmingly like our stockbroker.

I had a second problem with Barb's new hobby: To in-sure accuracy, the taking of the temperature had to occur at exactly the same time every morning. For some reason I couldn't fathom, Barbara selected 7:30 A.M. No problem dur-ing the week; I was up by then. But Barbara's graph did not recognize weekends and holidays.

Okay, you say. So she woke you up a few times. No big deal in the scheme of things. And okay, so she'd wake you up every night when she remembered to shake the thermometer down so it would be ready for the morning.

But what about the times I'd return to my office after a meeting to find one of those pink message slips with a note that said "Your wife called. She's fertile. TONIGHT!" Once, an office crony added an extra note: "If *you're* busy . . ."

There were a number of factors in my favor during these trying months of trying:

1. I had been on a diet, since it had occurred to me that I hadn't seen the scale register below 200 since I'd last worn bell-bottoms. I'd already reduced from 236 to 210 when Barbara read somewhere that diets tend to reduce sperm count. This got me wondering what I'd look like at a svelte 110 or so. (I eventually got down to 188 before I decided I'd rather have a baby than give up pizza forever.)

2. It was revealed that I was not the ideal baby maker after all. It seemed I had an abnormal number of abnormal sperm, a fact discovered by means of a distasteful test that included masturbating before work and leaving the semen in the refrigerator for Barbara to take to the lab. (For days afterward I refused to use salad dressing.) I was not upset by this lack of virility; the abnormality of my sperm was not surprising. After all, the lab probably had never before seen so many of the little guys doing the backstroke.

3. As a final ally in my antibaby crusade, I had my job. It seemed that business trips frequently coincided with Barbara's windows of fertility. I swear I had absolutely nothing to do with the timing of these trips; there were no payoffs to the account executives who arranged them or to the clients who demanded them. In fact everyone at the office knew about Barbara's pursuit and about my opinion of it, and they all sided with Barbara. I think it was because they had a sadistic desire to see if I really disliked kids as much as I said. Nevertheless Barb was at the point of considering tactful but threatening phone calls to the child-hating account executives who would call me on these egg-wasting excursions; she was convinced I had arranged a conspiracy.

My wife began wondering aloud why having babies seemed to come so easily to those who did not want them (teenagers and members of various ethnic groups). I explained that there was probably no statistical validity to this assumption.

"I'm sure there are many more teenagers who don't have babies than teenagers who do," I argued. "They just don't have a statistic for teenagers who don't have babies."

"Bullshit," Barbara replied, and quite eloquently, I must say. She was clearly not in the mood for such a conversation.

Meanwhile, Barbara had embarked on a campaign to make the most of however many normal sperm she could get out of me. An onslaught of articles and books revealed any number of old wives' tales and folklore regarding increased chances of pregnancy. It was not uncommon during this period to find her standing on her head after lovemaking or involved in an extensive search for mucus.

She had also developed a complicated regimen of abstention for a week before fertility and every other night during; this was to allow for a buildup of the normal sperm troops. None of this yielded any results, however, and her doctor was now allowing for only another month or two before bringing out the fertility drugs.

This was a prospect that terrorized me. Hardly a day went by without an article in the *New York Post* about quintuplets in Omaha or triplets in Bergen County, all allegedly the result of over-achieving fertility drugs. And while the thought of one baby was simply unattractive, the idea of a bevy of babies was enough to give me severe cramps. I immediately ended the backstroke lessons.

Thanksgiving was approaching: ten months of wasted eggs. I was back up to 221 pounds. The doctor told Barbara she herself had killed a month by misreading her graph; she had requested a screwing at the dip rather than on the rise.

In what I thought was a desperate move she bought a fertility testing kit. This consisted of three test tubes, a few different solutions, a medicine dropper, and, rather optimistically, a coupon for a pregnancy test kit. For one week, Barbara had to perform a series of chemical tests on her urine every morning. She was becoming the Dr. Frankenstein of fertility. The whole thing wouldn't have been bad, except that she would wake up before me, urinate, and then come back to bed, so I would frequently find a glass of urine (which looked not unlike our mouthwash) next to the toothpaste.

On Tuesday, I got the call at the office. "It looks like Thursday," she said. "Be ready."

Thursday, of course, was my poker night, but to bring that up at this juncture would have been to risk the addition of the fertility test solution to my coffee. I didn't have to bring it up, however, because, predictably, an account executive called not ten minutes later to inform me we would be flying to San Francisco Thursday afternoon.

"You're kidding," I said. "Barbara didn't even want me to come to work on Thursday."

I swallowed hard as I called home. Barbara asked for the telephone extension of the account executive in question. She was angry—hell, she was really pissed—because not only was another month killed, but also she had spent forty bucks on the damned test. I lamely suggested a solution — something about storing my semen in the refrigerator and a chicken baster — which only elicited increased wrath.

On Wednesday morning, following a very uncomfortable evening at home, I received another call. "I may let you live," Barbara announced. "It turned color today."

This, I knew, meant all systems were go for that evening, mission control having moved the launch up one day. I left the office at five o'clock sharp, turning aside an invitation to a late meeting with a terse, "Sorry, got to go screw."

And that night we made a baby.

Chapter 2

THE GOOD NEWS

OR

"Are You Absolutely <u>Sure</u> You Did the Test Right?"

The News

I slept late the day after Thanksgiving. The turkey dinner had been at Barbara's parents' house in Oceanside, Long Island, and had included a generous helping of baby-making discussions. I was growing increasingly apprehensive about the fertility drugs looming before me, and every once in awhile I'd catch myself thinking about whether or not we'd have to buy matching outfits for the twins.

When I woke up that day at about nine thirty, Barbara was long out of bed. I wandered out of the bedroom to find her watching Phil Donahue.

"Morning," I said, and presented a quick, precoffee kiss.

"Hi, hon," she replied.

I wandered into the kitchen for a mug of caffeine.

"My temperature stayed up," Barbara called.

Our apartment is laid out so that it's difficult to hear living room conversation from the kitchen. So I poked my head around the corner. "Huh?"

"I said my temperature stayed up."

"Oh." There were two factors at play on my side of this rather mundane exchange:

1. I had come to take for granted Barbara's personal weather reports.

2. I must admit to never having fully understood the whole temperature thing in the first place. I mean I knew it went up and down, but I was never quite sure of what meant what.

So I went back to the kitchen to add milk and Sweet 'n Low to my coffee.

Seconds later I joined Barb in the living room. I plopped down on the couch, placed my mug on a coaster, and lit a cigarette. "What's Phil up to?" I asked.

"Did you hear what I said?" Barbara asked.

"Sure. Your temperature stayed up." I smiled. I had passed the test.

"Did you *understand* what I said?"

I was beginning to come to the realization that something significant was happening.

"I think I'm pregnant."

I put my cigarette in the ashtray. Here were my immediate thoughts: A woman who desperately wanted to become pregnant and had been trying for ten months to do so had discovered, nearly two hours earlier, that she appeared to have finally succeeded. Upon learning this, she had gone to the kitchen, ground coffee beans, made coffee, gone out for the newspaper, and settled down with Marlo Thomas's husband.

I decided to vocalize some of these thoughts: "Why didn't you tell me?"

"I didn't want to wake you."

I now had a new thought: For six months, my wife had awakened me at 7:30 A.M. every weekend morning so she could take her temperature, and the one morning she had good reason to wake me up, she decided I needed my rest.

I hugged her. "That's great. Are you happy?"

"Yes."

At this time, it would be appropriate to point out that Barbara is a fairly conservative person. I understood that she was reserving her celebration until she had confirmation.

I, on the other hand, was genuinely happy. Yes, that's right. I was glad the ordeal was over. I was ecstatic that the specter of the dreaded fertility drugs had been removed. And I was elated for my wife.

"Did you call your mother?" I asked.

She shook her head. "I want to take this test first." From a paper bag, Barbara produced a home pregnancy test. I didn't ask if she'd used the coupon from the fertility test.

The suspense was killing me. I wanted to tell people. "So go ahead, take the test!"

"I can't till tomorrow."

This was very frustrating. Our telephone was demanding to be dialed.

Spreading the News

The next morning, Barbara took the pregnancy test, which was suspiciously similar to the fertility test. A drop of this, a drop of that. Then, blue urine.

"Is that what's supposed to happen?" I asked.

"Yes."

"So you're pregnant, right?"

"According to this."

"Great. Let's call your parents." (My parents, by the way, were on vacation and would return on Sunday.)

"Let's wait till I see the doctor."

To me there is absolutely no joy in knowing something unless you can tell somebody about it, which is why I'm not a great person to tell secrets to. "But you can't call the doctor until Monday."

"Uh huh."

"And he may not even be able to see you on Monday."

"What's your point?"

I admire Barbara for her patience. I really do. It's probably the only reason she can live with me. But on this particular occasion, it was driving me crazy. "Isn't that test 98 percent accurate?" I asked. She nodded. "So can't we call your parents and say 'We're not totally positive, but we're pretty sure we're pregnant'?"

"I don't want to get their hopes up," she argued, but I could tell I was wearing her down.

Fifteen minutes later, she was dialing and I was in the bedroom, listening excitedly on the extension phone. Her father picked up. There was some small talk. Then Barbara told him.

"Oh, that's very nice," he said. I stared at the telephone.

Barbara's mother got on. "That's terrific," she said. Notice the absence of exclamation points.

I couldn't contain myself any longer. "Aren't you excited?" I screamed. "You're going to be grandparents!"

"Certainly," Mom said. "But let's wait to hear what the doctor says."

Apparently it was genetic. Barbara's entire family would have made great Buckingham Palace guards.

It fact the only person on Barbara's side of the family who seemed excited was her youngest sister's boyfriend, Gary, who virtually lived at her parents' house in the room with the foldaway bed. Gary, whose impending engagement to sister Karen was assumed by all, seemed thrilled at the idea of being an uncle. I told him I wasn't sure he'd fit in with the family unless he learned to control his emotions.

I began trying my parents Sunday afternoon and finally got them around nine that night, which is why automatic redial is a nice feature, especially now that you have to dial an area code for Queens.

I calmly listened to them talk about their trip, which as always turned into a saga of my father's continuing difficulties in using a camera of any kind. I knew the photographs would bear this out: My parents' vacation album consisted mostly of long shots of nothing discernible and pictures of my mother in bathing suits taken from angles that always seemed to add unnecessary and unwanted emphasis to her thighs.

Their tale ended, as always, with the fact that there were still two unused shots on the roll, which meant that my mother would be taking pictures of the furniture again.

"We think Barbara's pregnant," I said flatly.

After several seconds of loud whooping noises, they said they wanted to hang up so they could run out to the bank and start a trust fund for the baby's college education. This was more like it.

Barbara and I vowed not to tell anyone else, not even the wire services, until the doctor confirmed the home test results, which he did, mercifully, the next day. Barbara informed me at work, adding that the doctor had predicted, with the certainty of a weatherman (at best, something between an educated guess and a shot in the dark), August 6 as the delivery date. Armed with corroboration from the medical community, we set about calling our parents again. I decided we had used a good system: It's nice to relate great news twice.

I called my grandparents. A phone conversation with them is usually about as exciting as a bad opera (or a good opera, for that matter) but, thankfully, is always a good deal shorter. In fact I've never managed to finish a cigarette while I talk to them. My grandparents are also not very demonstrative; their emotional responses generally run the gamut, as someone once quipped, from A to B. In this case, however, they seemed genuinely pleased, as near as I could tell, at the prospect of being great-grandparents.

Next I went on tour from office to office to announce the news among my colleagues. These were people who had suffered through ten months of the soap-operalike drama of our baby-making attempts, as well as my steady stream of anti-baby jokes. As a whole they took on a bemused expression when exposed to my impending fatherhood—somewhat like the expression they get when I write a headline that contains a particularly bad pun.

Monday evening I took off for Florida to shoot a TV commerical. We often shoot commercials there in the winter, for the obvious meteorological reasons. I was traveling with one of my favorite account people, Elizabeth, who, as irony would have it, was the same account person who had assigned me the San Francisco trip. When I told her the news, she acted like a tremendous weight had been removed from her shoulders.

While I spent the week in Florida waiting for it to stop raining, Barbara, I knew, would take care of telling everyone we knew and probably some people we didn't know. By the time I got home Friday night, there was only one person left to tell.

My best friend, David—an Australian (he talks funny) who is eleven years older than I am, wants a baby, and has a wife, Mary Ann, who doesn't (I had offered once, in jest, to switch spouses)—had spent the past ten months in great anticipation. During this period, every time we had dinner, he expected us to tell him we were pregnant. In fact at a dinner back in October I had said, "I think I'm going to Florida in December," and he thought I had said, "I think I'm going to be a father in December." Ignoring the fact that this would have meant a gestation period more suitable for rodents, David had circled the table and hugged Barbara and me before we could straighten out the misunderstanding.

So on Saturday night we went to the Italian place across the street. Although pleased, David was not as excited at the news as you might expect, given his earlier histrionics in reaction to a simple trip to Fort Lauderdale. This lack of enthusiasm could of course be attributed to the removal of the surprise factor: I had made him cancel a fishing trip to Canada in order to go to the neighborhood Italian restaurant. He was happy enough to pay for dinner, though, and that probably makes the whole experience of conceiving more than worthwhile.

Absorbing the News

Okay. So Barbara was pregnant. So we told everybody. So what happened next?

All along we'd been treating pregnancy as an end in itself, and now that we'd made it, it was only the beginning.

There were only two immediate changes:

1. Barbara was in a much better mood.

2. I became a more reliable poker player, no longer dependent on the state of my wife's fertility.

It was about two weeks, however, before the pregnancy really began to make itself apparent through slight alterations in our life-style. Those were a strange two weeks, a sort of limbo state during which I waited for some proof of my new father-to-be status. For a couple of days, I would catch myself staring at Barbara's stomach, as if she were simply going to inflate before my eyes.

Meanwhile Barbara had determined that there were no maternity shops anywhere in Greenwich Village and that most juvenile furniture stores are located either in Brooklyn or on Avenues A and B in Manhattan. The former was murder to get to; the latter was easy to get to but might result in murder since "Alphabet City" is a neighborhood you don't enter unarmed.

It was as if we'd been notified that there was going to be an earthquake in our apartment in ten seconds. Here was something that was going to change our lives profoundly, but we couldn't do anything about it except wait for it to show up.

Barbara expressed the opinion that her being pregnant was a pretty good reason for me to stop making baby jokes, to which I replied that she really couldn't expect me to give up smoking and baby jokes at the same time. She therefore took it upon herself to initiate a behavioral modification therapy: Seconds after vocalizing a baby joke, I would be subjected to pain.

These jokes were not things I planned in advance, but were reflexive reactions to straight lines fed to me unwittingly by friends and acquaintances. It worked like this: David would say something like, "Hey, mite (that's "mate" in Australian), you'll have to have us over to dinner after the baby is born."

And the first thing that would pop into my head would be, "Certainly. How do you like your baby cooked?"

This would be followed instantly by a sharp ache in my left shoulder, the result of a lightning-quick karate blow delivered by my demure, pregnant wife.

It was the first indication that pregnancy can be dangerous.

Chapter 3

THE FIRST MONTH

OR

"You Bought <u>Another</u> Book?"

---

*The Diet (and Why It Was Sheer Luck
If Somebody Happened to Give Birth to
a Normal Kid Back in the Old Days)*

Long before all Barbara's clothing had elastic in it, and very long before we both discovered that we didn't know how to breathe properly, and even before Barbara started going to the bathroom every three hours, there were the changes that were dictated by the doctor: a long list of dietary dos and don'ts.

Top of the list: Don't smoke. We would both have to give up our cigarettes, Barbara for the baby's health and me because I was going to be very supportive of everything Barbara had to do (or else Barbara would get mad at me).

Barbara, in that cute little frustrating way she has, simply stopped smoking. I mean I came home from work one day and there were no ashtrays. Period.

I elected a slower approach that began with switching from menthols to regulars. I then quickly moved from regular tar to low tar to ultralow tar. The next stage was to quit buying cigarettes, a step that immediately involved all my smoking coworkers. An art director whose office was terribly near my own finally resorted to taping a pack with my name on it to his door. Three months into my wife's pregnancy, I was down to three or four cigarettes a day, and none in front of Barb, unless we happened to be with somebody who was smoking anyway, in which case I smoked as many as I could until I got a dirty look from the person I was grubbing from.

Also on the doctor's "don't" list were saccharin and aspartame, which meant that anything low calorie was out, which meant that the elastic clothing would be in before I could say "Are you eating *again?*" The doctor also eliminated caffeine, and Barbara quickly searched out all the restaurants in the neighborhood that served brewed decaf. I maintained my preference for regular, but in the house I went along with Barbara, and it really didn't matter anyway because what, after all, is coffee without a cigarette.

There were a few more subtractions (like alcohol) and some additions (lots of milk and fresh veggies). All in all I began admiring Barbara for the sacrifices she was willing to make to have this kid and make sure it was healthy.

The Book Phase (and Why I Figure to Make a Lot of Money on This Book)

By far the biggest change during the first month was in our home library. Shelves that had once been devoted to trashy romance novels now carried enough birthing manuals to make you wonder how the human race survived before the printing press was invented. At one point a full inspection of the apartment uncovered the following titles (and some of them were library books, replacements for other, already perused volumes):

1. *Methods of Childbirth.*   This was an intriguing title, but a quick inspection of the contents did not reveal any methods I hadn't heard of, like having the baby exit through the mouth, or giving birth to a three-year-old,

toilet-trained, computer-literate whiz kid, or having the baby on a reverse Foster Parents Plan, through contributions from a poor family overseas.

2. *Childbirth with Love.* This was subtitled *The Complete Guide to Fertility, Pregnancy and Childbirth*, a claim that Barbara evidently did not believe, at least not enough to make her discard the other nine or ten books in the house. In fact, as if to lend credence to Barbara's lack of faith, the next book I found was called . . .

3. *The Complete Guide to Pregnancy.* I found the contents of this book to be a bit strange chronologically, as the chapter on "The Normal Changes of Pregnancy" came before "The Diagnosis of Pregnancy." This seemed to imply that the sudden addition of forty or fifty pounds was likely to be attributed to another cause. Another chapter was called "The Common Discomforts and Nuisances of Pregnancy," and I couldn't help feeling that somehow husbands were included in its pages.

4. *Husband-Coached Childbirth.* This 1965 classic by Robert Bradley, which was donated by relatives, included expert advice for all kinds of pregnancy-related situations like this one:

> You may be walking down the street with your wife when she suddenly lets out a yelp, bends over, and holds her side. . . . Don't try to make her keep walking but steer her over to the shop window and have her bend down to act very interested in something in the window. After a few moments, the round ligament spasm will let up and she can comfortably walk erect again.

In the first place, when confronted with pain, my wife does not yelp. Yelping is something a puppy does. The sound that would come from my wife in this situation would be much closer to that of a full-grown puma with its leg caught in a steel trap.

In the second place, even before women's lib I don't think all that many men would try to make their wives keep walking when the little women were yelping, bending over, and holding their sides. ("Shirley, I said *keep walking!* No rest time for twenty minutes! Mush!")

In the third place, I doubt that Barbara, while in the grips of a painful spasm, would be all that interested in convincing passersby of her fascination with the live lobsters in the fish store window.

And finally, my wife's walk, even prior to her pregnancy, was not so much erect as a ducklike waddle.

5. *The Birthing Book.*   This volume promised to show the mother-to-be how to have an easier labor and delivery. I could tell from the first chapter, "You Have to Love It: Life on the Labor/Delivery Floor," that they were on the right track. My primary advice to expectant mothers would also be to get up off the floor and onto a bed. Labor's bound to be less painful that way, and doctors work better standing up than they do on their knees.

6. *Pregnant and Loving It.*   The cover blurbs of this book included "Could you give me hints to cut down on my caloric intake?" Hell, I can do that. Get back on the saccharin and aspartame!

7. *The First Nine Months of Life.*   This was by far the most medical book of Barbara's collection. It included pictures of our-child-as-a-tadpole, and got me wondering if the Sears portrait studio really takes them that young. (The tadpole did not seem to be photographed against a blue sky backdrop, however, and the picture did not appear to be mounted on a wooden plaque.)

8. *Big Apple Baby.*   This guide to raising a child in the big city included a section on restaurants. Personally I don't intend to let my child pick the restaurant until he or she is at least two years old.

There were other books, I'm sure (I didn't delve too deeply into the kitchen). In fact the day I got the idea to write this book, Barbara saw this chapter in the outline and sheepishly admitted she had brought two more books home from the library that day. And what was really scary was that she hadn't even started with the pregnancy exercise books yet.

Discussions: *Where to Put the Baby*

When you live in a one-bedroom apartment, there is no obvious answer to the question "Where will the baby go?"

A brief description of our apartment here: There is a narrow entry hallway by the front door (when you think about it, really the only topnotch place for an entry hallway), which brings the guest (or anybody else who happens to come in) to a small alcove with a desk customed-designed to hold our personal computer and all the hardware and software that goes along with it. Next to that is Barbara's Lucygraph, a large, black apparatus that is used by art directors to decrease or increase the size of images. Then comes the doorway to our pride and joy, the new kitchen we put in when we bought the place, which includes a dishwasher and microwave oven, which I never quite figured out how to use without having something explode. A right turn from the kitchen puts you in the living room, a 12-by-20-foot behemoth with a low wall system along one wall, a sofa bed, a coffee table, a folding dining room table, and a drawing board, which we feel is an essential accessory for any living room. Included in the list of furnishings is my antique radio collection, or, more accurately, that portion of it that does not fit into the hall closet, since Barbara has determined that a 1941 Philco doesn't go with our black, gray, and white modern decor. Another narrow passageway leads to the bathroom and a 12-by-15-foot bedroom outfitted with a platform bed, a dresser, and a couple of storage trunks that we use to stash either my fat wardrobe or my thin wardrobe, depending on what state my nearly continuous dieting is in.

Hence the question: Where will we put the baby?

My answer was to put it in the bedroom with us, but Barbara pointed out that my alarm clock would wake it up in the morning. She suggested that we divide off the part of the living room closest to the window, but I said then she wouldn't want to run the air conditioner because the baby would get a draft. I refused to have a little thing like a baby deprive me of air conditioning during a New York summer.

Barbara then came up with a compromise position: one crib in the living room for nights and one in the bedroom for days. I refused on principle to have two cribs in a one-bedroom apartment.

Our friends from down the hall, Fran and Rick, stopped by, and Rick, who's an architect, had a great idea. "Why not install a Murphy crib?" he said.

I immediately got behind this idea. "Barb, it would be terrific." She looked at me dubiously. "We fold the crib out at night, and the baby sleeps. Then during the day, we fold it back into the wall, and the baby's gone. Night comes; wheeee, there's the crib, there's the baby." Barbara gave me a Bruce Lee chop, and I suddenly yelped in pain and doubled over with a spasm in my side. I went over to the bookcase and pretended to look at the titles on a low shelf.

David and Mary Ann came over a few days later, and David kindly inquired after the neighbors. "Did the old people next door get out of town yet?"

As I have said David comes from Australia, where they throw midgets for fun and eat a vile stuff called Vegemite, so I expected that from time to time he would say or do something that more civilized people would consider to be in bad taste. Because I had known him for eight years, I hardly noticed these things, but I knew they bothered Barbara, so I often pointed them out to David.

"David, that's a terrible thing to say," I admonished. "The people next door happen to be very nice."

"I wish they'd get the hell out already," Barbara said with a gleam in her eye.

This rather distasteful attitude on the part of my wife and best friend was caused by the knowledge that a move by our elderly neighbors to a Sun Belt state, or anywhere else for that matter, would result in the sudden availability of an adjacent one-bedroom apartment that might be purchased relatively cheaply. We could then break through a wall and create a two-bedroom, two-bath palace, with plenty of room for an office as well.

David, who lived in a loft space he had designed himself and had gone through the whole business of hiring contractors to build it, began speculating about what it would take, besides the sudden mobility on the part of our neighbors, to build this monstrous apartment. He ran off the names of carpenters, electricians, and plumbers he could recommend and started adding up ballpark estimates.

"You know, David," I interrupted, "I don't think we'd even need to break through the wall."

"No?" he asked. "Why not?"

"We'll just buy that apartment for the baby. We'll have the first newborn in Manhattan with its own co-op. It can live in there with a nurse, and we'll go visit every once in awhile. We'll bring a bottle of milk; it'll be nice."

The last word was punctuated by a rather expressive groan on my part, as I had been jabbed neatly in the ribs by my wife. And I had managed to get that far in my comment only because Barbara had been in the bedroom when I'd started.

This ongoing discussion about space highlighted one of my major baby phobias. I knew that we'd eventually figure out someplace to put the kid for a year or two, but after that we'd have to move the little one out of the hall closet or wherever we had stashed him or her.

This meant that we were committed to moving to a bigger place within three years, and I shuddered to think what a two-bedroom apartment in Manhattan would cost. I didn't want to have to move to Brooklyn, Queens, or, gulp, New Jersey as that would mean I'd have to wait until nine or even ten o'clock on Saturday night to get the Sunday *Times*.

With typical ungrounded optimism Barbara assured me that everything would be fine. This is her job in our marriage: I am the worrier, she is the one who says "Everything will be fine." So far she has been right more often than not, but worrying gives me something to do as I do not use drugs. Worrying is cheaper.

Discussions: *What to Name the Baby*

One topic that had entered our conversational repertoire even before Barbara became pregnant was baby names.

I was an early proponent of Woodrow, as a son named Woody Hallen was virtually irresistible. Barbara did not share my enthusiasm, however, but leaned toward a legion of overly popular *J* names, like Jennifer, Jonathan, Jason, Joshua, Jessica, and Justin.

I vetoed each one of these with a selection of my own: Mel, Steve, Debbie, Ethan, and Alan.

These were all dispatched with equal haste. I had her pretty hot on Valerie for awhile (Val Hallen had a nice ring to it), but this, too, was eventually discarded.

Barbara then went through a soap-opera phase, and every night at dinner I was bombarded with Alexis, Crystal, Brooke, Solange, Erica, Zane, Felicia, Britta, Dimitri, Dr. Voight, and other names that seemed to dictate the wearing of low-cut gowns or having an affair with the wife of a first cousin.

The next hot name was Heather, a Barbara selection that I was against, as the name called for a tall, thin girl with long, ash blonde hair, a paisley skirt, and a guitar.

We then became avid followers of TV and movie credits,

or any medium that provided a long list of names that we could call out to each other like immigrants learning to pronounce English. For a long time it appeared certain that our offspring would be named after a gaffer or a best boy, until I got us out of the habit by telling people we had decided to name our child Technicolor.

Perhaps we were actually hampered by a lack of restriction. We didn't need to name the baby after a relative, except for its Hebrew name, which no one would use or be able to pronounce or write. My Hebrew name, for instance, is something like Meyer Rachmael, but I've never tried to sign a check with it (and I choke myself every time I try to say the Hebrew *ch* sound, which comes from the depths of the throat and always brings up a mouthful of phlegm). Anyway, without having even a first letter dictated to us, we hopped all over the nameworld without finding anything that sang to us.

Until one day when I happened to come up, from nowhere in particular, with Corey for a boy and Casey for a girl, and we decided to rest a few months before starting on middle names.

Discussions: *What the Baby Will Be Like*

Barbara is short, I'm of average height. Barbara has freckles, I have thick lips. Barbara has reddish hair, I have brown hair, but my beard, when I have it, is red. Barbara has brown eyes, I have green eyes. I have a tremendous sense of humor, Barbara has the good sense to laugh at my jokes. I have my mother's fat thighs, Barbara has good-sized boobs. I'm a writer, Barbara's an artist. We both wear glasses.

Using our limited high school biology knowledge of dominant and recessive genes, we tried to figure out what our kid would be like. We decided it would wear glasses. It would be artistic in some way, but not musically, as our living room radiator has more musical ability than either one of us. Barbara said she hoped the baby would have my color eyes. I said I hoped it wouldn't be a carrot top, as people with that real orange hair are almost always incredible nerds.

Barbara professed not to have a gender preference. I, too, played this question on the fence, though I leaned slightly toward a girl.

Our fathers, however, had definite opinions in this matter. Barbara's father, Stan "the Man," had sired three girls and wanted a grandson. My father, Bernie "the Photographer," had put all of his efforts into raising one wonderful son and wanted a granddaughter. Our mothers seemed ready to take on whatever showed up.

My friend David wanted a boy. This was because David is an avid fisherman and has always been disappointed that my experience as an outdoorsman goes no further than peeing behind a tree in Central Park during a softball game. I enjoy fishing if we can sit out on a lake in a boat, and the fish don't bother us much. David will put any body of water under siege with a massive appropriation of equipment. I think bait is icky.

David thought that he could convince Mary Ann to have a child soon after we had ours. Our sons could then join him on his fishing trips, while I could teach them baseball.

"It'll be great, mate," David said. "They'll grow up together, play together, all that."

I had other ideas. "Our kids won't play together," I said. "I won't have my kid coming home one day and saying, 'G'day, mate, how 'bout a Vegemite sandwich?'"

"Yeah, well where else is your kid gonna learn how to throw a boomerang?"

I had to admit it; I could not, even at this early stage, bear to deprive my kid of boomerang lessons. I told David they could play together. Mary Ann, who had joined us by this time in our conversation, just sort of winced.

"What am I going to do, mate?" David asked. "Mary Ann doesn't want to have a baby."

"You can have ours," I offered.

Luckily Barbara wasn't with us at the time.

Chapter 4

THE FIRST TRIMESTER

OR

"Honey, Didn't You Just Go to the Bathroom?"

Why a Pregnant Wife Is Nature's Way of Giving You Practice in Caring for a Baby

A baby, when it is first born, does only four things, all of them extremely well. It cries, it eats, it sleeps, and it pees. These are also the four main functions of a woman during the first trimester of pregnancy.

Yes, your newly pregnant wife will cry. And laugh. And yell. Often within seconds of each other. I'm told these mood swings are caused by hormonal imbalances, but to me they're worse than PMS. I mean at least PMS is predictable. You know that your wife will hate you for a couple of days each month. These pregnancy mood swings make the poor, unsuspecting husband think he's walked into an amateur acting class and there's a drama coach yelling to a student: "HAPPY! SAD! ANGRY! HOMICIDAL!" And the student, of course, is his wife.

Barbara would periodically go through all those emotions and more during the course of a ten-minute conversation, so that at times her side of the discussion would sound like: "Oh, honey, I had such a terrible day. My client was so dumb and OH BY THE WAY I HAVE A BONE TO PICK WITH YOU.

WHY THE HELL DO YOU HAVE TO MAKE THE COF-
FEE SO STRONG IN THE MORNING? So do you want
to go to a movie tonight? I don't feel so good. I love you."

I was not completely unprepared for this. Alan, an account
person at work who has a two-year-old daughter he speaks
of very highly, had warned me to watch for emotional mood
shifts. "Be understanding," he had said. "Be loving. Stay as
far away from her as you can."

Of course, I could never be fully prepared to see my wife
turn into a Meryl Streep movie. But I thought I coped rather
well. As soon as I saw one of these moments coming on (signaled by an imitation of an old Jewish woman: "Oyyyyyyy"),
I decided I had to go to the bathroom, which I did with a copy
of the thickest book I could find. I'd come out in about fifteen
minutes; by then, Barbara was guaranteed to be eating or fast
asleep.

I had heard the expression "eating for two," but Barbara
seemed to be eating for Lithuania. One Saturday afternoon,
I wandered into the kitchen to find her preparing about two
dozen of those little cocktail franks—rolling dough around
tiny hot dogs and popping them into the toaster oven. I knew
we were going out to dinner with Fran and Rick that night,
so I figured Barb had invited them over for hors d'oeuvres first.
This, however, was not the case. Barbara was making lunch.
For herself.

I decided to fix myself some popcorn (the one thing I had
learned to make in the microwave with relative safety). Meanwhile Barb removed the tray of wee wienies from the toaster
oven, put them on a plate with some mustard, and headed
for the living room. By the time I followed, about a minute
later, she had cleaned the plate and was already headed back
to the kitchen for a piece of cheese.

When I called her to task for this incredible gorging display,
she claimed weekend insanity.

"I don't eat this way during the week," she said. "During the week, I have yogurt for breakfast and a salad for lunch. That's all."

I mentioned that I didn't think this explained the box of Entenmann's donuts on top of the refrigerator. In response she farted.

This was not an isolated fart. Her farts had increased, not only in number, but in volume and odor, to a point I deemed excessive. In fact flatulence was not the only one of Barbara's bodily functions that was hastening to make itself annoying.

I remembered that one of the reasons I was relieved when Barbara had announced her pregnancy was that I would no longer be awakened at 7:30 A.M. on weekends for the ritual taking of the temperature. This had, indeed, turned out to be true. However, I was now awakened at least twice every night of the week for the taking of a piss.

This I was told was the result of some sort of hormonal thing. Later on it would be caused by pressure on the bladder, but now it was a hormonal thing. I thought it was time Barbara got her homones under control. When I told her this, she hiccupped. I told her she was really going to seed. She belched. I told her the least she could do was say "excuse me." She started singing some tuneless song of her own invention.

And another thing. My wife had decided to alter her relationship with her environment. I mean she seemed to relate to certain climatic conditions, say heat or cold, in a way that seemed to have little or no connection to reality.

I took a day off from work in January to do some writing at home and wandered out of the bedroom in the morning to discover that my living room had apparently been transplanted to Minneapolis.

"Isn't it a little chilly in here?" I inquired.

Barbara looked up from her iced coffee (decaffeinated, of course). "No," she replied.

I went over to the wide-open window and brushed the icicles off the blinds. "I'm not used to having a windchill factor in the house," I said.

"It was stuffy."

"Stuffy? We could hang sides of beef in here!" To this remark there was no response, and so I sat down at the word processor with my down jacket around my shoulders.

About an hour later, I noticed that drops of sweat were making the keyboard sticky. I turned around to find Barbara curled up in a blanket.

"Warm front from the south?" I asked.

"What do you mean?"

"Barbara, the furniture is perspiring."

She looked up from her raspberry tea. "It's my body temperature," Barbara explained. "It's staying up, so I get hot and cold."

I thought I was finished hearing about her body temperature. But I was determined to be tolerant, so I hung my scarf up in the closet and made no further comment.

During the next few weeks, it was a regular occurrence to find Barbara cozied up in a down quilt and asking me to open the window. Never before had we had so much weather in our apartment, and I hope we never do again.

I don't want to make it sound like my lovely wife was unbearable during this period. That absolutely wasn't the case. Much of the time, she was asleep.

I understand that pregnancy is probably very tiring for a woman. Add to that the fact that Barb woke up two or three times a night to go to the bathroom, and you've got a really good reason for a midafternoon nap and a ten o'clock bedtime.

I figure this is nature's way of preparing an unsuspecting couple for the arrival of its little creature. By the time August 6 rolled around we would be quite used to waking up in the middle of the night and conking out during the day.

If, in fact, we made it to August 6. It was going to be a long nine months.

Why You'll Hope Sex Is Like Riding a Bicycle

No matter what you may have heard, pregnancy is not conducive to sexual relations. This should not come as a surprise, considering the rapid and unpredictable changes the woman's body is going through. But just in case the implications of the last section escaped you, here is a list of why you can expect your life to become somewhat monklike in regard to sex:

1. You never know when your wife will fart, need to pee, or fall asleep.

2. In the middle of sex, your wife is likely to get hungry.

3. *You* are likely to fall asleep since you were up all night listening to your wife go to the bathroom.

4. Sex may be interrupted by five minutes of hysterical laughter, which your wife will undertake for no reason that you or any other rational human being can fathom. This may be followed by three minutes of intense sobbing and a desire for Cheese Doodles, by which time you'll remember that you really wanted to do a crossword puzzle anyway.

5. For some reason I never understood (and you'd be amazed at how many things about pregnancy no man can ever understand), being with child also means being with dry skin and an itchy body, to the point where I wanted to give Barbara a necklace from Hartz Mountain. Where once the removal of clothes had been a prelude to lovemaking, it was now the start of a scratching orgy. No part of her body was left unscratched, and the lightning-fast movement of her hands made any attempt at foreplay dangerous at best. She would roll over so I could do her back while she barked

directions: "LEFT! UP! RIGHT! HIGHER! HARDER! HARDER!" Remember, these were only scratching directions. (We ran into our pregnant friends Meri and Joe and mentioned Barbara's propensity to remove her bra at night and make concentric cricles with her fingernails to relieve the itching. Meri, who was in her eighth month at the time, seemed downright joyful at this revelation. "You do that, too?" she exclaimed. "It feels so good just to set them free at night!" Joe and I stared at each other as the girls chuckled to themselves; apparently there were going to be some things that would just make us shrug our shoulders and sigh.)

6. Although Barbara wasn't showing much yet, I was constantly thinking about getting into positions that might harm the baby. This was not in itself a deterrent, except that anything on my mind during sex, other than speeding freight trains, was, in fact, a deterrent.

More Discussions: What to Name the Baby

One night I came home from an ordinary day at work and we called for our usual order of Chinese food (dumplings, orange beef, sesame chicken), which we do once a week like good Manhattan yuppies. The yuppie's union requires in its bylaws the ordering in of Chinese food once a week (once a week we also have to eat Lean Cuisine). I tell you this by way or relating the supreme ordinariness of this particular day, so that you'll know how unprepared I was for Barbara's conversation opener as we extracted the aluminum tins from the bag that had just been delivered.

"What do you think of Brad Hallen?" she inquired innocently, as if she was asking my opinion about an author.

Keep in mind that for two months I had been having open and frank discussions with a belly named either Casey or Corey. Which is why Barbara's query left me speechless.

"You don't like it?" she asked.

"What happened to Corey?" I replied.

She kind of winced. "I don't know. I'm starting not to like it."

"What if your mother called right now and said, 'Your father and I decided we don't like Barbara anymore. We're changing your name to,'" I paused here for effect, "'Georgette.'"

"What are you talking about? The baby's still seven months away."

"Well, I don't like Brad. Brad Hallen. No rhythm. We need a two-syllable name. One-syllable names are no good."

"What about Mark?"

This was a remark I should have seen coming. How could I explain that my parents, by their own admission, were not expert baby namers, that, in fact, they had almost named me Ricky Mickey instead of Mark Richard?

Instead I made something up: "That's different. The Mark and the Hallen blend together because of the hard *k* sound. The *d* in Brad makes you pronounce the *h* in Hallen: It doesn't roll off the tongue." I took a deep breath, proud of my inventiveness.

"Bullshit," Barbara said.

Recognizing a losing battle, I retreated to the position of postponing the discussion until I could do some research.

My research was not what one would call scientific. For the next week, I wrote down every name with which I came into contact. I began with my book shelves at the office. Unfortunately, most of the books at my office are authorless reference books, but this did not deter me. A dictionary yielded both Webster and Noah as possibilities. Another book, published by Doubleday, brought to mind Nelson and, being as I am a baseball fan, Abner. I had an almanac published by Simon and Schuster, so Simon went on my list. After a moment's thought, I decided to leave off Roget.

Then I looked at a photographers' index and listed Tom, Rick, Nicholas, Richard, David, Dennis, Barry, Bruce, Chris,

Pierre, Jan, Sal, Craig, Hal, Walt, Chuck, Ed, Gozo ("Gozo" was the entire listing; I wasn't sure if it was a first or last name), Moshe, Ted, Jung, Ryuzo, Nick, and Tohru. I then crossed out all the names that were shared by people I knew; I didn't want anybody thinking I had named my kid after him.

I then turned my attention toward celebrities: Mick, Sylvester, Dustin, Robert, Michael, Charles, Luke (I had recently seen *Star Wars* on cable), Arnold, Marcello, John, Paul, George, Ringo, and Sting.

Later I looked at the roster of my beloved Mets: Wally, Lenny, Darryl, Dwight, Howard, Gary, Rafael, Keith, Ron, Roger, Jesse, and Danny. After a period of deliberation, I added Mookie.

The research department at my agency contributed a list of the ten most popular names of 1983. I ignored this completely, as I was determined my son would not have an overused name.

At week's end, my "research" had created a list of seventy names, everything from Aaron to Zachary. True, many of these replicated ones we had rejected during our movie credit phase, and true, some of the names on the list were "throwaways" (Barbara was not likely to select a name like Conan for our son), but I was confident that my list would provide a viable alternative for Brad.

I proudly handed my compilation to Barbara. "Hmmm," she mulled. "Alexander. Alexander Hallen. That's not bad. Alex Hallen." And so it seemed for a moment that our son would be named after a character on *Family Ties*.

I sighed. I could live with it. And then Barbara said, with absolutely no provocation, "How about Matthew?"

I grabbed my list and scanned it. Matthew was not on it, but I did remember it. It had been on that list of ten most popular names, number two or three if I recalled correctly. I bristled at the prospect of a most popularly named son.

"Come on," I said. "I have better names here than that." I glanced quickly—okay, frantically—at my list and read at random. "How about Adam? Algernon? Ansel? Benedict? Barnaby?" There had to be a better name on my list than Matthew. A week of work could not go for naught, particularly since I had taken the trouble of alphabetizing. "Cornelius!" I cried. "Derek. Dylan. Emanuel." I was fading fast. "Fabian?"

"Matthew," announced Barbara. "Matthew Alexander Hallen."

Either I was just growing weary or the name was growing on me. In the end, I acquiesced. Matthew Alexander for a boy, Casey Alexandra for a girl.

I now knew what to call Barbara's stomach.

Chapter **5**

THE SECOND TRIMESTER

OR

"Are We Going Camping? Uh, Sorry, Nice Blouse, Dear."

A Scary Week in February

The week before Valentine's Day, Barbara went for her regular visit to the doctor. Afterward she excitedly called me at the office to tell me that she had heard the baby's heartbeat, albeit with extreme amplification and the doctor saying, "Hear that? That's it."

"The doctor asked me where you were," she said, "and I told him I didn't know we were going to hear the heartbeat today. It goes 'brump brump' really fast, like it's panting."

I told her the baby had probably been out jogging.

"Next week is the sonogram," she said. "I want you to come to that."

That night, she told me about other things that had transpired at the doctor's. Her weight was okay. He told her she didn't have to bother exercising. And, to Barbara's great relief, he had informed her that he wasn't antipainkiller.

Now, according to my mother, the only way to have a baby is while totally unconscious. Mom wouldn't have it any other way. She also wouldn't want to have Dad in the room with her.

But in our new age of husband-coached natural childbirth, some doctors, it seems, refuse to prescribe any painkiller whatsoever. Barbara's friend, Meri, had one of those doctors, so Barb had been really apprehensive about the drug question.

"He said the goal was not to use them," she told me, "but if there's considerable discomfort, he doesn't hesitate to use them."

"That's great," I said. "What about for you?"

"Very funny."

"What about for me?"

Later in bed she told me the sonogram would be the next Wednesday. I had been thinking about that, and although I'm certainly no expert on pregnancy, or anything much else for that matter, it seemed to me that it was a little early in the term for submarine technology. I told Barbara all of this.

"Yeah, well, it *is* a *little* early," she said. "But the doctor thinks my stomach might be a little too large."

"I thought you said your weight was fine," I said.

"It is," she assured me. "It's just that my belly is a little too distended. Too large."

"Too large for what?"

She grinned sheepishly. "One baby."

I thought I took this news serenely, although our downstairs neighbors later disagreed. Something about primal screaming.

"It's still only a slight possibility," Barbara said.

"We only have one set of names. What are we going to do?"

"There's really probably not more than one," Barbara said.

"My parents only started one trust fund. Only one of them is going to college."

"The doctor said we could always sell one of them." She saw my eyes brighten. "He was kidding."

"No, no, it's a great idea. We sell one of them now for, say, $50,000. Then in twenty years we'll get them back together, and there'll be a big article in the *Post*: 'TWINS, SEPARATED AT BIRTH, MEET AGAIN!' Then we'll sell the movie rights."

"Forget it."

"Why not? That way they can both go to college."

By the next morning I had decided not to get upset about

it until we knew if it was true. And besides it might not be so bad. If Barbara was going to insist on two kids eventually, which I figured she probably would, we might as well get it over with all at once. I just hoped they wouldn't be identical; I didn't want a pair of twin imps playing little tricks on their father all the time.

A couple of days later at work I told my constant advisor, Alan, that twins were okay with me.

"You don't want twins," he said definitively, as if the subject were herpes.

"I realize they'd be a lot of work," I replied. "But I'd rather get it over with."

"No, no, let me explain." He made himself comfortable on my office couch. "You see, a young baby is like silly putty with aspirations of someday being a human being. If you put it down over there"—he pointed at a spot on the floor—"it stays there. It will not move. It will cry. It will eat. It will wet. But it will not move."

He took a deep breath. "But soon it will move. It will crawl. All over. It will find your gold Cross pen. It will unscrew the cap. It will write on your leg. You cannot reason with it.

"I love my daughter very much, but I would not want two of her. Take my word for it. No twins. And I don't think you have to worry about it. Caroline's doctor said there was that possibility, too, and the kid came out at just over three pounds. I think they just do it to get paid for an extra sonogram."

"Thanks, Al, I feel better now."

"Twins." He made a kind of shivering sound and left.

Wednesday finally came, and off we went for our sonogram.

If you ever want to get an idea of what Ellis Island was like in the old days of immigration, just visit Beth Israel Hospital in New York. It was as if there was a sign on the front door that said, "Give us your poor, your humble doctors and nurses." The United Nations, up the block, could not have boasted as many different nationalities.

Barbara, her bladder brimming to the top, led me to the radiology department where we were signed in by the Jamaican receptionist and told to wait to be taken to the sonogram department. The East Indian sonogram receptionist told Barbara to drink a few more glasses of water and to inform her when she was "uncomfortable." I knew this would not be long, as Barb was already standing as though her legs were pinned together at the knees.

Three glasses of water later, Barbara informed the receptionist of her discomfort by emitting a low, moaning sound. The receptionist, in turn, used her delightful accent to inform Barbara that there were no rooms available; it would be a few more minutes. Barbara found that her belly prevented her from crossing her legs as tightly as she would have liked.

Eventually we were ushered into another room, where a Haitian nurse gave Barb a gown to put on. Then she was told to lie on a table next to a machine that looked like a combination video game, personal computer, and food processor.

The nurse spread some kind of goop on Barbara's stomach and aimed something that resembled an electronic vibrator at it. A pair of pictures showed up on the screen; the nurse pressed some buttons to focus.

And there, in almost perfect definition, was our baby.

Yes, *baby*. Singular.

It was amazing. Although it looked like a large shrimp, we could make out the head and the spinal cord. From a different view, we could see the heart beating like a car's turn signal. From still another angle, we could see the arms and legs.

It was moving. A lot. It raised its arm and scratched its head to indicate, I guess, prenatal dandruff, as well as a tendency to take after its mother. It was virtually doing calisthenics. And while the screen did not indicate relative size, the fact that Barbara was not yet feeling any of this movement indicated just how tiny this thing was.

When it comes to the abortion issue, I was, and still am, prochoice. But if you wanted people to think twice before having an abortion, all you'd have to do is require a sonogram before the operation. In the fourth month, at least, there is no doubt the fetus is alive. The image on that computer screen is unforgettable. Especially when it moves.

And the Indian doctor, after instructing the computer to perform various measurements, told us that our baby was perfectly normal. But she refused my request for ten wallet-sized photos.

I spent the next few weeks with my ear glued to Barbara's stomach, listening for the heartbeat I had seen so clearly. All I heard was what seemed like a mighty river filled with frogs.

Our baby was not yet ready to be detected by the naked senses. Barbara, however, was ready for some Di-Gel.

Things Start Taking Shape

I suspect that taller women are somewhat better at being pregnant than shorter women. My wife is a shorter woman.

When I say this I don't mean better at handling the baby part of pregnancy. Barbara followed her doctor's orders precisely, eating all the things she was supposed to (and a lot of them), not eating any of the things she wasn't supposed to, visiting the doctor regularly, reading all those books, and so on. She was an ideal mother-to-be.

Where lack of height is, if you'll excuse the expression, a shortcoming, is in the area of appearance during pregnancy. A tall woman, say five foot eight, who is normally in good shape, retains enough of her lithesome grace so that it seems like there's this cute little bulge in her tummy. These women unknowingly incurred Barbara's wrath whenever they made the horrible mistake of crossing her line of vision.

That was because Barbara, who *is* normally in good shape, but is only five foot two, was beginning to attain a figure that could only be described as spherical.

Not only was she exhibiting a ballooning in the front, but

she was also bulging in the rear, an indication, according to some old wives' tale she'd heard, that she was more likely to be carrying a Casey than a Matthew. (This fit into a prediction we'd already made based on our estimate of when conception had occurred—something about the sperm with the Y chromosome lasting longer, so that if you conceived earlier in the fertile period it was more likely to be a girl. We figured Casey's sperm was hanging around waiting for the egg to show up.)

Anyway, back to Barbara's figure. What was happening to her appearance was not her fault. Although I've made fun of her seemingly continuous eating habits, she had gained the normal amount of weight (according to her doctor) for approximately halfway through the term. However her lack of longitude accentuated her newly acquired latitude to the point where, as we sat watching television one evening, she turned to me and asked, "Am I rotund?"

Usually, this type of question begs for an answer like, "Rotund? You? Why, dear, you have the figure of a gazelle. Whatever would make you even suggest such a thing?"

Unfortunately this sort of reply would have been Nixonian in its obvious falseness. For one thing, our favorite activity for the past month or so had been watching her belly button disappear. Secondly, at the very moment she had asked the question, Barbara had been straining to rock herself forward enough on the couch to reach the remote control on the coffee table.

So I had to resort to, "I think *rotund* might be a little harsh, dear. How about *adorably round?*"

After some interrogation, it came out that *rotund* was a word Barbara's mother had used that afternoon. And while criticism of any kind was always taken to heart more when it came from a parent (as opposed to a less-knowledgable party like, say, a husband), comments concerning her figure were certain to bring about short-term depression.

"You're pregnant," I said reassuringly. "You're supposed to be, um, big."

"I *am* rotund, aren't I?"

I was missing too much of "Hill Street Blues" to make this conversation worthwhile. Besides, I had quickly identified it as one I could not avoid ending up on the short end of, since it was evident that the discussion would not be over until I admitted her rotundity, at which point I was bound to be severely rebuffed.

"You're beautiful," I said. "You're glowing," I said. (This was true, although I believe the effect was being caused by a fire engine passing in the street.) "I love you."

She allowed herself to tilt back in the sofa, indicating that she was willing to accept my last comments as an indefinite conclusion. I felt proud of myself for my shrewd maneuvering.

But during the next commercial break, I heard a grunt and looked toward the couch to see Barb staring at her stomach.

"Barbara," I said, "your fifth month of pregnancy is no time to start worrying about your figure. You've got four months to go yet."

This was, perhaps, the wrong thing to say.

"I'm going to look like a bowling ball with little legs coming out of it," she said.

"The doctor said your weight was good," I reminded her, trying desperately to change direction. "And remember, you read that you'll lose three times the baby's weight when it's born."

"Where did I read that?" She was puzzled but hopeful. I was sure she'd told me she'd read it, but the old wives' tales were coming in so quickly that it was hard to keep track of them.

"Maybe Alan told me. Caroline is nice and thin again."

This did not cheer her up. Caroline was one of those awful taller women who hadn't looked that bad pregnant. "Even if that's true," Barbara said, "what are the chances the baby will be eighty pounds?"*

---

*This was an exaggeration; she had not gained 240 pounds. I hasten to say this as my wife will, at some point, read this book.

"Probably nil," I replied. "But if it *is* eighty pounds, we'll name it 'Refrigerator.'"

Barbara smiled at this reference to the Chicago Bears defensive lineman and heaved herself out of the couch to waddle into the kitchen for something to eat. And I was able to watch the rest of "Hill Street" in peace.

Barbara's stomach and rear end were not the only parts of her body that were burgeoning. Her breasts, which under normal circumstances are somewhat larger than anything the citrus family has to offer, were now approaching the magnitude of advanced weaponry, to the point where I felt sure the Russians would include Barbara's boobs in arms negotiations.

This had already necessitated the purchase of several new brassieres, which, after the baby was born, could be brought along on picnics and strung between trees for an after-lunch nap.

These mammoth mammaries contributed to Barbara's large, economy size appearance and fostered the hope that our offspring would have a voracious appetite.

Barbara was sufficiently upset about her new figure that she ignored her doctor's advice and bought an exercise videotape. It had, said the cover, been designed by doctors (as opposed to, I assumed, a well-known actress) and was, therefore, supposedly safe. A viewing of the tape seemed to bear this out, as the exercises consisted mostly of stretching. In fact most of the stretching was being done by the leotards worn by the pregnant women who performed the exercises. Imagine if you will an assemblage of Bosc pears dressed in multicolored tights trying to touch their toes. You will then know why I laughed when I saw the tape.

"It's not funny," Barbara said.

"Oh, come on now," I argued. "Forget you're pregnant for a minute and look at it." I pointed at the screen.

"Okay. It's funny."

The videotape soon fell out of use anyway, as Barb realized the only exercise she really needed was getting in and out of chairs.

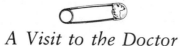

A Visit to the Doctor

In March I agreed to join Barbara on one of her monthly excursions to the doctor. It was a revelation.

The office was in a loft building in the East Village, and upon our arrival we discovered that the passenger elevator was out of order. The freight elevator was working, however, which was good because I was of the considered opinion that nine stories was too far to expect a pregnant woman (or her husband) to climb.

When we emerged from the freight elevator, Barbara's doctor was there to meet us, which I thought was a nice personal touch until he got in to go down, explaining that he had to, as he put it, "go grab a baby." We would be seen that day by his partner.

The waiting room was like any other, except for the two children playing with Lego blocks on a miniature desk. A number of pregnant women sat reading magazines or exchanging stories about their various discomforts. Barb immediately joined one of these discussions while I stared at stomachs.

After awhile, a woman come in with a bundle and proceeded to remove six or seven layers of clothing from it until it was revealed to be a baby. She said a few words to the receptionist, was told the doctor could not see her that day, and got ready to reassemble her son.

This was a truly amazing process.

First she spread a blanket on the floor of the waiting room as if she were going to have a picnic. She then put the baby on it as if he were going to be lunch. The kid lay motionless on his back and made gurgling noises. She tickled him. His legs moved up and down. She cooed to him. He cooed back. This was all the preliminary to the main event.

She lifted him up and sat him on her lap while she put on him a hat that looked like a World War I flying helmet. The kid looked at me with the same expression I usually save for clients who are demanding unreasonable revisions. Then came the layers: jumpsuit, sweater, jacket, overcoat. Mom then hoisted up the finished product by grasping him firmly under the arms.

The kid looked like a scarecrow. His arms were outstretched to the side, his legs spread-eagled in midair, feet pointing away from each other. No limb was movable; he might as well have been clothed in plaster of paris. She inserted him into a front-loading holster so that he had no choice but to lean into her bosom looking like an extremely small airplane that had somehow crashed into a large structure.

She then retrieved a number of bags containing, I assumed, an assortment of baby implements and angled her way out the door so that bags and baby's still-extended arms and legs made it through without damage.

It was all adorable.

"That was cute," I told Barbara who, along with all the other expectant mothers in the room, had been watching the drama with fascination.

"*You* thought a baby was cute?" Barbara asked, as though I had informed her of my decision to become a Hare Krishna.

"Don't tell anyone, but I think I'm starting to get into this whole thing."

"Does that mean no more jokes?"

"Don't push your luck."

The doctor held a brief conference with us, during which he gave explanations for all of Barbara's various aches and pains. These, he said, were a result of ligaments and muscles being stretched in ways they'd never expected and were a perfectly normal part of pregnancy.

He then put a little electronic thing up to Barbara's stomach so we could hear the baby's heartbeat. And sure enough, it went "brump brump" just as Barb had promised.

Finally, he noticed that the shape of her belly included a clifflike dropoff above the belly button, which indicated to him that the fetus was a week or two farther along than we had thought.

"I'd say end of July instead of August 6," he announced.

This was not particularly upsetting to me, as I had not made any specific plans around August 6, other than to warn my secretary that it would behoove her to stay away from me around then as I was bound to be a nervous maniac.

"That was fun," I said to Barbara on the way home.

"I told you you'd like being a father."

"It may be fun being an expectant father. I reserve judgment on actual fatherhood."

"Oh, I can just see you holding the baby in your arms for the two o'clock feeding and making little goo-goo noises while it eats."

"Two o'clock feeding?"

"Uh huh."

"A.M.?"

"Yup."

"No way."

She sighed in exasperation. "Look. I want the baby to have one bottle a day to get used to it. It'll eat every four hours or so. So you can do the two o'clock or the six o'clock."

"What about the ten o'clock?"

She thought about it. "Oh, yeah. Well, maybe."

I suddenly realized I had been manipulated. By getting me into a discussion over *when* I would feed the baby, she had skirted the whole issue of *if* I would feed the baby.

I was about to bring this up, but Barbara had pulled up short and was doubled over in pain. She even yelped. I was at a loss for what to do, as we were on a residential block and there were no store windows handy. I led her over to the nearest building and told her to pretend she was examining a brick.

The spasm was brief. But, of course, by then I had forgotten all about the feeding conversation.

Fathers-to-be really have to be on their toes.

What Every Mother-to-be Will Be Wearing This Year

It seems to my admittedly male mind that getting pregnant is quite a lot to go through just to be able to get a new wardrobe.

Back in December, when Barbara's stomach was only a shadow of its future self, I gave her, as gag gifts, two stereotypical pregnancy shirts that said VIP IN PRODUCTION or some such nonsense.

That was the beginning.

Soon afterward the new clothes started coming in dribs and drabs. First there were the pants with the three snap closures so that the waistline could grow right along with Barbara. Then there were a couple of shirts that Bubba Smith would have felt comfortable wearing. Then the pair of jeans with the front panel made entirely of elastic. Then the extra, extra, extra large T-shirts. The only place I've seen more Xs than there were on the labels of these shirts is on posters for porno movies.

Then came the mass invasion.

Barbara, who laughs at me when I buy chic antique ties and sports jackets at used-clothing stores, visited a couple of cousins in Brooklyn and came back with enough outfits to start a maternity shop. But, alas, only winter clothes. The summer outfits came from another cousin on Long Island. Then I noticed that a store in Manhattan named Reborn Maternity was having a big sale and was moronic enough to mention it to Barbara. That produced a few more items.

On top of all this, another alarming trend was beginning: Barbara was starting to wear my clothes.

As our closets began to fill up with these new duds (and it didn't take many of them to fill up a closet), Barb tried to console me with the promise that, after the baby was born, I would inherit lots of the unisexual kinds of stuff like sweatshirts. This was of limited consolation as she was wearing my favorite sweater at the time.

And that was of very limited consolation to her because it fit.

I should point out here that the abundance of clothing wasn't exactly unnecessary. Even under normal circumstances Barbara is not a neat eater. She has never seen fit to give her mouth exclusivity as far as where the food goes is concerned. She often likes to share her meals with others, so that when she eats lobster at a restaurant, everyone else has to wear bibs, too. And not just at our table. I mean everyone else in the restaurant!

But as Barbara grew bigger, the odds of her getting through a meal without dropping something on her attire increased in direct proportion to her anatomy. After a meal, it appeared she had wrestled with her food more than devoured it. She didn't have a lap to put a napkin on, and she couldn't get close enough to a table so that the table could catch anything that was dropped. Even if she was eating standing up, anything dropping straight down from her mouth would land on her chest or stomach.

So, take this tip, men. When your wife goes out shopping for maternity clothes, make sure she buys a smock, too.

The Baby Is Heard From

One of the biggest mistakes an expectant father can make is to assume that there will be no interactions with the baby until after it is born.

As I have mentioned, very early on I found myself talking

to Barbara's stomach. But I was not the only one engaged in conversation with Barbara's anatomy. I would, at times, come out of the bathroom to find Barb in the living room talking out loud to no one visible. In bed we both spoke to the baby, whom we called C.M. after both its possible initials.

What does one say to a stomach, you ask?

"Hi, C.M., it's your daddy speaking."

"C.M., did you see what your daddy did?"

"C.M., did you hear about that trade the Mets made?"

"C.M., did you see what Alexis did on 'Dynasty'?"

And so on.

Our families were not immune to this silliness either, and visits were bound to elicit, at minimum, a series of greetings directed at Barbara's midsection, as if her stomach had arrived independently and had a seat reserved for it at the restaurant.

There was some rationale for all this. Studies* have shown that fetuses can hear sounds and will be more comfortable after they're born with sounds they've heard often while in the womb. That is why some pregnant women wear headphones on their stomachs and play classical music. I figured I would make Barbara sit near the TV during telecasts of Mets games so the baby would get used to hearing the announcers' voices.

So everyone spoke to the baby. Which was all well and good . . . until the baby started talking back.

Well, not actually talking. But it was making itself heard nonetheless.

As you might expect, Barbara was the first to feel it. Not real kicks, but definite movement. She said it was a fluttering kind of feeling, the sort of feeling you get before your first real date.

I could put my ear to her tummy and hear the fluid being pushed around. I could tell when the baby was awake and when it was sleeping.

---

*I've only heard about these studies; you'd be surprised how little actual research I did for this book. Or maybe you wouldn't.

Somewhere in the fifth month, it really started moving. We'd be lying in bed, about to start snoozing away, and Barb would suddenly yell, "Go to sleep, C.M." Then she'd grab my hand and put it on her stomach and after awhile I'd feel the little punch or kick. Just a soft little pop, but then I was on the outside. I can't imagine what it must feel like to have a miniature Muhammad Ali sparring with the inside of your body.

There is, of course, nothing that can be done about this phenomenon short of Barbara's swallowing a pair of booties and some tiny boxing gloves and hoping for the best. We both knew it would get worse, too. (We'd heard stories of actually seeing the outline of the baby's foot or fist through the stomach.)

Our kid, good yuppie-to-be that he or she was, seemed to have taken a liking to Chinese food already, as the ingestion of fried dumplings and orange beef would bring on a performance of Swan Lake. The hypothesis that this was a result of MSG proved false when the cook at the restaurant swore none was used, so we had to go on the assumption that the kid enjoyed Szechuan more than any other food.

"Oooh," Barbara would say. "Baby's up."

"Knocking on the door," I would remark.

"Oooh," she would say again, and shove my hand on her stomach.

And there were still three months to go.

A Brief Tribute to a Terrific Lady

You may want to skip this section. It's not going to be funny, and I sincerely hope it will offer no information you can use during your pregnancy.

On March 10, Barbara's mother passed away after a long and valiant battle with cancer. She was fifty-five.

No one was surprised that she fought the disease as hard as she did. Inge Tamarkin had had to be brave since she was a girl.

She was born Ingeborg Levi in Germany at precisely the wrong time to be a Jew in Germany. The family escaped from Germany before most of the horrors began, but they lived through the terror of the blitz in England.

Later in America she shortened her name to Inge. She met and married Stanley Tamarkin, and they loved each other for thirty-three years while they raised three beautiful and loving daughters. She and Stanley quickly became Mom and Dad to me when I married Barbara, and their other daughters' selections, Roy for Gwen and Gary for Karen, were adopted just as quickly into the family.

It was a bit of culture shock for me, an only child, suddenly to have three sisters and two brothers, but the family was and is so close that it taught me what I missed as a child and what I have to look forward to as an adult.

The end came at a bad time (not that there ever could have been a good time): The first grandchild was on the way; Gwen and Roy were about to be married; and Karen and Gary were about to be officially engaged.

The three girls shed a storm of tears—for Inge, for their father, for themselves. Their mother would be missed beyond imagination, especially at this time when motherly advice would be so sorely needed. But their first reactions were to rally around Stanley while Roy, Gary, and I rallied around them. There was a lot of rallying even while there was so much crying.

The night after the funeral, Barb was in bed, her head on my chest, trying to keep her tears under control (although the doctor had said that, as far as the baby was concerned, it was okay for her to be upset). Helplessly I stroked her hair. It was, Barb told me, what her mother used to do when Barbara was a girl and crying about one of the things girls cry about.

I think it's one of the best things a mother can ever do.

And, by the way, if the baby was a girl, she would be named Casey Ingrid.

Chapter 6

THE THIRD TRIMESTER

OR

"You Want Rhythm? Get Ringo Starr in the Delivery Room With You!"

Why Pregnant Women Should Stay Out of Coffee Shops

By the sixth and seventh months, Barbara's stomach had already expanded beyond imaginable capacity and, when nude, she was beginning to resemble a Buddha. I could no longer hug my wife unless I invited friends over to help. It looked as if she had swallowed a basketball, and it often felt as if the kid were dribbling it.

The kicks were getting stronger, and the excitement of seeing the little indentations in Barb's belly had already worn off. She'd lie in bed at night, her shirt pulled up, going "Boop boop. Boop boop." I quickly came to understand that this was her way of adding sound effects to the kicks, although I was never quite sure if this was for her benefit or mine. I told her that the baby would soon be making enough sound by itself, thank you, and that she should stop helping it. "Boop boop," she replied.

Barbara had invented another little routine at night. I had to say "Goodnight, C.M." to her stomach, then put my ear to it to see if our child was awake. More often than not, I would be rewarded with a swift kick to the side of my head. I didn't know if

I should be happy about this, knowing that my offspring was already responding to my voice, or annoyed that my wife and child appeared to have formed a conspiracy against me.

The point of all this is that the sixth and seventh months of pregnancy are acutally pretty boring. Nothing much happens. The baby was not planning any milestones in the near future, and it wasn't time to shop for furniture or start breathing classes. It seemed like the steamroller of impending parenthood had stalled.

This is probably nature's way of letting you catch your breath before the final onslaught of delivery and the subsequent insistence of a child to be around you at all times. I figure the sixth and seventh months are kind of like the benches they put on the staircase in the Statue of Liberty.

Now you're probably thinking to yourself, "Hey, I'm reading this section because I'm intensely interested in why pregnant women shouldn't go into coffee shops, and you're talking about the Statue of Liberty. What gives?"

Well, okay, if you insist. Barb and I went to a movie one day, and were shocked to find there was no line. We habitually get to movies about an hour early because there's always a line, but this time there was no line. So we had an hour to kill. I suggested we go into the Greek coffee shop (in Manhattan, that phrase is redundant) for a snack. We walked in and ambled up to the counter. And encountered a problem. Not only could Barbara not squeeze between the stools to get to the counter, there wasn't enough room between the counter and the stool for her stomach.

Which is why pregnant women should stay out of coffee shops.

The First Baby Gifts

We went to my parents' house for dinner, an excursion we dreaded, as my parents live in a tucked-away portion of Queens that is virtually impossible to get to from Manhattan unless you take a helicopter.

We sat in the living room as my father presented his latest acquisition: a $450 camera that he had been promised was more automatic than any of the previous ten or so automatic cameras he had owned. With great pride, he demonstrated all the little warning beeps the camera could make and all the little instructions that showed up in the camera's computerized window. He then admitted that not only had he not figured out how to use the camera, he hadn't even figured out how to read the instruction booklet.

Meanwhile Barb and I had been looking through one of their photo albums, and both of us burst out laughing. On one page was a photograph of nothing but water, which my mother had adroitly labeled "Aruba, 1977." On another page was a photo of a tiny person on a beach in front of some bungalows, with what seemed to be a few miles of water between the model and the photographer. We wondered aloud if my parents had taken separate vacations and my father had snapped the picture from another island.

"You don't need another camera, Dad," I said. "You need to learn how to choose your subjects and frame a picture."

"He needs to have his head examined," my mother said.

Some pages in the album confirmed my mother's lack of confidence in Dad's photographic ability. She had bought postcards and trimmed the borders to make them look like snapshots.

"I'm going to use this camera for the baby," Dad said. "I want perfect pictures of her." My father was convinced we had a Casey on our hands.

"Well, keep practicing, Dad. You've got three months yet."

Dad frowned as he put the camera down and Mom handed Barbara a small white box. Inside was a little white knitted sweater and cap.

"I hope it fits," Mom said. "I haven't knitted in years."

I don't know what it is that makes relatives knit. I imagine it's one of those primal things that has remained in our subconscious from the days before there were other ways to obtain clothes, like from a store.

"It's adorable," Barbara said.

My mother beamed.

About a month later we saw my parents again and received two more gifts. My fanaticism about baseball being well-known, everyone had been on the lookout for tiny baseball mitts so I would be able to give my child an early start. Everyone knew my child would play baseball regardless of gender.

And that's why my mother presented us with a tiny pair of boxing gloves that squeaked when you squeezed them.

Now I knew my parents were aware of the difference between a baseball glove and a boxing glove. So there was bound to be a good story behind my parents' apparent desire to see their first grandchild become a pugilist.

Well there wasn't.

Oh, there was a story, all right, but not a very good one. My mother had mentioned to one of her mah-jongg cronies at the swim club that she had been searching for a miniature mitt. This lady excitedly declared that she had spotted just such a mitt and vowed to procure said item. The next day she showed up at poolside with her little package already gift wrapped. My mother, her curiosity running rampant, unwrapped it as soon as she was home, only to discover that her friend seemed to think that Larry Holmes was a first baseman.

"I didn't have the heart to tell her," my mother said, handing me a brown paper bag.

Inside was a baseball glove and ball that my mother had located on her own. The mitt was larger than the boxing gloves and didn't squeak. It looked like it would be good for a three- or four-year-old, which was okay, since it would have looked silly for my child to be playing baseball with a teething ring.

Now all I needed were teeny tiny cleats.

Why Floors Get Dirty

Around the sixth month of pregnancy, I began noticing an interesting phenomenon. I'd come home from work and find all kinds of stuff on the floor: paper clips, pens, Barbara's colored markers, mail, cookies, various scraps of paper, and so forth. If I ignored this field of junk, I'd come home the next night to a bumper crop.

Now I've never had any complaints about the neatness of our home. Although I think I'm fairly liberated when it comes to household chores, I admit that Barbara has always done most of the cleaning kind of work, primarily because, when I do it, she's never satisfied with the results.

Barbara has a long-time distrust of my cleanliness, a result of a visit to my apartment when we were dating. It was an experience she would always remember with horror (something about the antique eggs glued to my frying pan). Anyway, since we've lived together, Barb has taken it upon herself to do the cleaning, and I've never seen any reason to say, "Hey, there, stop hogging the mop!"

And while Barbara has never been a neurotic clean freak (like my mother who, for years, never allowed anyone in the living room so it wouldn't get dirty), no one would ever accuse us of living in a pigsty.

Until now.

"Barbara," I said one evening, "how come you're leaving all this junk on the floor?"

"Because," she replied, "when I drop something, I can't bend down to pick it up."

I looked at her and agreed with her plight. Anything at her feet would not only be out of reach, it would be out of sight. I agreed to harvest the floors every night after work.

The loss of visual contact with her pedal extremities was obviously weighing heavily on Barbara's psyche. Late one night in May, the seventh month, Barb and I were lying side by side in bed, naked, after another game of "find a position that works." Barbara was engaged in her favorite pastime, staring at her stomach and watching it move like something out of a horror movie. It was hard to imagine how the baby could get any bigger unless Barbara somehow grew an annex.

"Lie flat," Barbara ordered. I ignored her because I was never sure anymore if she was talking to me or the fetus. "Lie flat," she repeated, and gave me a little shove to cure my confusion. When I was satisfactorily flat, she asked, "Can you see your feet?"

I looked and was relieved to discover that, despite having regained just about every pound I had lost, I could see my feet.

"I can't," Barb announced. This came as no surprise, of course, as we had already determined that any area directly beneath her was a visual black hole. She began to raise her foot slowly. When it was about two inches off the ground, she said, "There. I can just see my toe over the horizon."

I thought *horizon* was a funny word to use, but when I put my head next to hers I saw that it was perfectly accurate. There was a definite horizon and her barely visible toe looked like it was about ten miles away. I said that I thought it was a neat optical illusion. She hrumphed.

I decided to try to cheer her up, so I put my hand right below her stomach, held up a couple of fingers so she could see them, and performed a kind of impromptu puppet show.

She was not amused.

Two Dumb Conversations

One night Barb announced, "We have to talk." That particular declaration brought back terrible memories from my single days, because then anytime a girl said, "We have to talk," it meant I would have to find a new girl. While I was much more secure in my relationship with Barbara than I had been with any of my girl friends, I still thought it was a lousy conversation opener and fully expected her to tell me she no longer liked the name Matthew.

"We need to decide whether we want to use a pacifier or not," she said.

My immediate thought was that some psychologist had decided that parents should stick things in their mouths as a role model for baby. "I don't want to use a pacifier," I said. "I'd rather smoke."

"I mean for the baby. Do we want the baby to use a pacifier?"

"I don't know. What's the alternative? Having it chew on my leg?"

"No, sucking its thumb." Apparently, something had been published regarding the advisability of having baby suck on something natural, like a manual digit, rather than something unnatural, like the pacifiers we grew up on.

Actually it seemed this was an important decision to make. Someone at the office clued me in: "Pacifiers have good and bad points," he told me. "The good thing is you can take away a pacifier. The bad part is you always have to have a spare pacifier with you, in case the first one falls on the floor and you can't wash it."

He continued: "We were lucky with our daughter. She got off the pacifier when she was two. Unfortunately, she started sucking her thumb when she was four."

I had a vague recollection of a thumb-sucking problem I had as an infant. I sort of remembered my mother putting some awful-tasting stuff on my thumbs to stop me from sucking them. Of course she also tried to feed me liver, and that didn't get me to give up eating.

Anyway I just didn't feel like discussing it when Barbara brought it up. So I said, "Do we have to decide right now? I mean, considering you're in your seventh month, we've got awhile yet before the baby starts teething."

That ended the conversation, but it got me thinking about more serious matters like: How Jewish did we want to raise our kid? Did we want to share our views on God? Did we want to censor what the kid watched on TV, especially cable? Did we want to enforce a bedtime? How much allowance would we want to give it?

After some thought, however, I decided that these issues, too, could wait until our baby was teething.

"Are we going to let the baby in bed with us?" Barbara asked a week or two later.

"Only if it's on your side," I replied.

Barbara's question had been inspired by still another article. I renewed my sincere wish that people would stop writing articles or that Barbara would stop reading them. I then pointed out to Barbara that it would surely be a year or more before the baby could join us in bed of its own accord, and thus tabled the discussion for a few months, or at least long enough to allow me to finish watching a "Honeymooners" rerun.

How Much Is That Baby in the Stomach?

One of the copywriters at the office, out of a desire, I guess, to torture me, handed me an article from the *Wall Street Journal* entitled "Expecting a Baby Soon? Expect to Spend a Pile of Money During the First Year."

The article listed various costs associated with surviving the first year of a baby, including a portable infant seat ($30), a portable crib ($110), a Snugli infant carrier ($53), a stroller (up to $260), an infant car seat ($40), an outdoor swing ($15), and so on. The article even got petty enough to mention plastic stoppers for electric outlets (99¢).

The article didn't bother us much. We would immediately save $55 on the car seat and outdoor swing by virtue of our not owning a car or having any outdoors (unless we wanted to put the baby on the roof).

We also weren't worried about furniture and clothing costs,

as we had discovered something much better than money or even credit cards.

Relatives.

In fact relatives from both sides of the family had gotten into a virtual bidding war over who would buy what. Aunts-to-be Karen and Gwen had received dibs on the stroller. Grandfather-to-be Stanley had the crib. Grandparents-to-be Sunny and Bernie had the layette (although I still had only a vague idea of exactly what a layette was). My grandparents were scrounging around for something to buy so we awarded them the dressing table contract. And Barbara's Aunt Ellen had even volunteered to pick up the tab for a week's worth of a sleep-in nurse.

Now, then, if only we could find someone to pay for that darned 99¢ outlet stopper.

It seemed like there were a lot of things we (or other people) would have to buy that our parents never had to purchase for us. In 1954 there were no such things as Snuglis or Sassy Seats, or designer strollers from Japan.

And there certainly weren't any video cameras.

No, our parents had to settle for nonmoving, nontalking snapshots of our babyhoods (or, in my family's case, various parts of my body in unfocused close-ups).

It should go without saying that, being good yuppies, Barbara and I already possessed a VCR, which we used to tape shows (many of which we never got around to viewing) or to play rented movies. ("We'll take *Citizen Kane, Annie Hall,* and *Hookers from Hell.* Yes, of course, we're members.") But with the baby on the way, Barbara wanted to be able to record on tape all the milestones in its life.

I had no objections to buying a video camera (although we have our wedding on videotape, and believe me, *My Dinner with Andre* is more exciting to watch), but I had no idea which one to buy. Did we want a basic, bulky VHS camera that was compatible with our VCR? Or did we want to keep up with technology and buy one of the new, streamlined eight-millimeter jobs? Did we want to be able to film baby's first steps in slo-mo? Did we want baby's first words to be crystal clear? Did we want to be able to tape baby's first birthday with only the light from the candles? Did we want to be able to edit, so that the final product would have only baby's good angles?

After hours of deliberation, I came to a decision. I would allow the baby a pacifier if it wanted one, but it couldn't come into bed with us.

News From the Doctor

On May 20, Barbara went to her doctor for a regular checkup. The fact that it was her doctor was significant because it was the first time she had seen him in months. This was because fate had dictated that all of her regular appointments had come when her doctor had been "grabbing babies," so she'd been seeing a lot of his partner.

Barbara's doctor took a look at the sonogram and announced that the delivery date would be July 27 instead of August 6. I didn't like the fact that he was moving up an important event like this on such short notice. This was a ten-day difference. True, we had been warned three months earlier by his partner that it might be the end of July, but this was Barbara's *real* doctor telling us—and with a definite date, too! I had been mentally preparing myself for August 6—could I be ready ten days earlier?

Of course there was a good side to this news. July 27 would be a Sunday; August 6 was a Wednesday. On a Sunday it would be easier to get a cab, there'd be less traffic, and I'd be more likely to be near my wife when It happened. On the bad side, I'd be more likely to be near my wife when It happened. I wasn't sure I wanted to be near my wife when It happened. Neither was she. We both knew the chances of my remaining calm while It was happening were about the same as the chances of the delivery date's actually being July 27.

Nevertheless, I marked my calendar.

Other People's Babies

It amazed me to realize how much interest I suddenly had in other people's babies. One Saturday I had to do some work with Alan, so I went to his house in Oceanside and had the chance to observe his daughter in her natural habitat. When there was no answer at the front and side doors, I went around to the back to find Alan with his wife, mother-in-law, and daughter doing yard work.

Well, actually, little Elizabeth was scampering around the yard with an old rake. Alan caught her and introduced us. "Hi," said Elizabeth.

"Hi," I replied. The conversation obviously over, she scurried into the house, leaving Alan holding the rake.

We went through the back door into the kitchen. I noticed a green blotch of paint magneted onto the refrigerator.

"That's her latest work," Alan told me.

"Frog?" I guessed.

"Elizabeth," Alan called to his daughter while spinning her toward the fridge. "What is that?"

"Lion." This was a definitive answer.

"How does the lion go?" Alan asked.

"Rrrrr," said Elizabeth, and ran into the living room.

"She sure runs around a lot," I observed.

"The energy of youth," said Alan. He looked tired.

The very next day, Barbara and I went elsewhere on Long Island to visit her friends Carol and Arthur and their son Jeffrey, who had recently graduated from his Gymboree class. Gymboree is a franchised operation where babies are organized into exercise classes while their mothers stand around comparing their offspring's abilities on, say, the big ball.

Jeffrey was asleep when we arrived, which gave me the opportunity to play with his toys. He had a playpen full of them, to the point where it was obvious that the playpen had become a holding bin for toys rather than an actual play area.

The first thing I tried was a little car dashboard with a steering wheel, turn signal, and gearshift. This caught my attention because I had noticed the identical toy in Alan's house the day before, and I wanted to see what made it so popular with young drivers. There was a big plastic key that turned the thing on. It made a growling noise that got louder when you shifted into second. The turn signal caused an arrow to flash on and off with a clicking sound. The horn beeped.

"Don't buy that toy for your kid," Carol called from the kitchen. "The noise'll drive you crazy." (For similar reasons, I had also been warned away from a game called Hungry, Hungry Hippos.)

Most of the other toys involved all kinds of gizmos that spun or flipped or made a sound. These toymakers had pulled out all the stops to get and hold a kid's attention.

"See all those toys?" Carol said. "He only plays with two of them. That's all you need. Two toys."

I knew that, although her advice might be sound, it would be impossible to follow as long as we had relatives.

My favorite toy of Jeffrey's and, as it turned out, his favorite, too, was a basketball set with a cardboard pole, plastic hoop, and plastic ball. We played one-on-one.

I won.

Carol took us into Jeffrey's room which was color coordinated to a degree I would not have thought possible. The wallpaper pattern appeared everywhere, so that at times you almost felt the room wasn't three-dimensional.

It made me sad seeing this room, because it was so nice and babylike and because our kid was just going to have a piece of the living room. How would this affect our child, I wondered. Would little Casey or Matthew end up as an addict, porn star, or accountant solely because he or she had been deprived of a color-coordinated nursery?

I was starting to think about looking at the Westchester real estate listings in the *Times*. Granted this was a few steps away from actually looking at the listings, much less traveling to Westchester to look at houses, but it still signaled a radical change in my thinking. Would I be willing to commute for my kid's welfare? Would my kid really be better off in the suburbs?

Well I knew one thing anyway. My kid was going to have a little basketball set.

In late May I spent a day shooting a commercial at Kaufman Studios in Astoria, Queens, which is the same place the Marx Brothers movies were shot, the same place Woody Allen shoots most of his films today. Shooting in this place is like playing a softball game in Yankee Stadium; exciting and a little humbling at the same time.

The client we were shotting with was the same client that had been with us in Florida back in December when I had first heard the news of my impending fatherhood, and the gang greeted me with a bunch of questions about how I was liking it so far.

Then one of the clients, Terry, told this charming little tale about her two-year-old:

For a few weeks, her son developed what can only be described as a nasal fixation. He loved putting things up his nose. One night he was sitting at his high chair, and she noticed he had a corn niblet up each nostril. She removed them only to find two more. The extrication of the second set of kernels produced still a third pair, and so on. Finally she had to take the kid to the emergency room for a nibletectomy.

A few days later, when she noticed that her son had apparently inhaled a bag of M&M's, she called the doctor.

"Plain or peanut?" asked the doctor.

"What difference does it make?" Terry said.

"If they were plain," explained the pediatrician, "there's no problem. They'll just melt."

"That's when I saw this stream of brown gunk flowing out of his nose," Terry said. "M&M's melt in your nose, not in your hand."

What's the moral of this story? Well there is none, other than the fact that Terry finished it by telling us how great her son was, so I got the feeling that being a parent must be pretty terrific if you can overlook a gunky nose.

Still I thought nose plugs might not be a bad idea.

On Father's Day, we visited Meri and Joe, who now had a two-month-old girl named Lauren. Meri and Barbara had had some apprehension about my seeing the baby because she was colicky, and the girls didn't want to expose me to the loud side of fatherhood. Their worrying was unwarranted, however, as Lauren was perfectly quiet the whole time we were there.

We watched baby Lauren sleep a lot, and suck her bottle, and get burped. When placed in her playpen, she tried valiantly to move. She crawled in place for awhile, but hadn't yet seemed to have figured out how to place one knee in front of the other to produce forward momentum. Then she tried to roll over, and although Meri swore that this feat had been accomplished, Lauren could not flip herself over.

The family had a great game that everyone enjoyed playing. It was called "where's the tongue?" Here's how it was played: Someone would hold Lauren on his or her lap, and everyone else in the room (on this day it was Joe and Meri's parents) would say, "Where's the tongue, Lauren? Come on, let's see the tongue." The rules of the game required that this request to see Lauren's tongue be repeated continually in many variations and in a falsetto until coincidence dictated that Lauren actually revealed said organ, at which time it was pointed out to all spectators (in this case, Barbara and me) how intelligent Lauren was.

Later on, with everyone else out in the backyard, I had a quiet moment with Joe in the living room. He was holding his tiny daughter, who virtually disappeared in his burly arms.

"She doesn't seem to do much yet," I said.

"Oh, you'd be surprised," Joe replied. "She's very good with bodily functions. Stuff comes out everywhere. She's great at vomiting. You wouldn't believe the distance she gets. It's like Old Faithful."

"Do you change her and everything?"

"Sure. I really should change her now, but as long as she's sleeping, I'm holding off. When you change her, that's when the floodgates really open."

"So you're enjoying it?"

"Oh, yeah." He yawned. "If I could only stop falling asleep."

That Fourth of July weekend was part of the much-ballyhooed Liberty Week, and with millions of people pouring into Manhattan for the festivities, we did the only logical thing: We went to Long Island. Barbara's dad, along with Karen and Gary, had gone to Lake Tahoe for the week to scout out time-shares, so we had the house in Oceanside to ourselves.

Now before you say, "How nice, a weekend at the beach," I should point out that Oceanside has neither a beach nor an ocean and was named by someone who was decidedly not bothered by minor details.

Over the weekend, we had David and Mary Ann and Alan, Caroline, and Elizabeth over for a nice suburban barbeque. This gave us the chance to observe Elizabeth in action for a prolonged period of time.

Elizabeth arrived fast asleep, a condition that was corrected all too soon. Alan and Caroline took turns eating while the other one fed, held, and generally pacified the two-year-old. Ice cream was something she could handle by herself, and I do mean handle as Elizabeth apparently viewed her spoon as a not entirely necessary piece of apparatus. Neither, I may add, was her mouth; it appeared she believed that ice cream smeared on her face would be ingested by osmosis.

Dinner over, the fun really started. Elizabeth discovered that a plastic parsons table made a fine drum and began beating away. When the legs came off, she complained to her parents that "my drum broke," but was perfectly capable of reinserting the legs herself.

"That's a table," Caroline said.

"Drum," said Elizabeth.

"It's a table," insisted Caroline in the hopes of giving her daughter a reality check. "You're just using it as a drum."

"Don't lean on it," said Alan. "You'll break your drum."

"TABLE!" glared Caroline.

"Daddy, let's run," was Elizabeth's next request, and she and Alan headed off to the grass where they proceeded to scamper about in no clear pattern.

"The terrible twos," Caroline told us.

"How long can she keep this up before she gets knocked out?" I asked, hoping the answer would be ten minutes or so.

"Six, maybe eight hours."

I gulped and looked over at the lawn where Alan was collapsed on the grass. "Let's run more," said Elizabeth.

"Daddy's tired," said Alan.

"Why?" asked Elizabeth.

"Because I can't run around as much as you can."

"Why?"

"Because Daddy's older than you are."

"Why?"

Alan looked up at us helplessly. "This is the 'why' stage," he pointed out needlessly.

"Let's run more," said Elizabeth.

"Oh, Jesus," said Alan, getting up with a groan.

I decided that I might have an unavoidable business trip in two years and that it might very possibly last twelve months.

So That's What a Layette Is

In late May Barbara, my mother, and one of Barb's cousins went shopping for a layette. I waited with anticipation to hear the results of this excursion, because, as I have said, I really didn't know what a layette was.

I know that probably sounds dumb. But to me a *layette* sounded like a single object, maybe a piece of furniture. Looking at the word itself, it seemed obvious that a *layette* was, simply, a small *lay,* since I knew well from doing crossword puzzles that *ette* was a "diminutive suffix."

We had already purchased a dressing table. That was easy. It was exactly what you'd expect a dressing table to be: some drawers with a top on which one could dress a baby. The crib had been bought, and, although I hadn't actually seen it, I didn't anticipate any surprises there. Some cousins had even dropped off a cradle, which was presently lying disassembled in our bedroom, and this seemed like everything I though a cradle would be, except that I couldn't find a "bough." I was worried about a bough breaking because I knew that that would cause the baby to fall, cradle and all. However, the cradle came with a handwritten sort of sign-in sheet with the names of all the babies in the family who had slept in it, and I figured if the bough had survived all of them, it would make it through ours, too.

So, then, what the hell was a layette?

"A bunch of baby stuff," Barbara informed me. Ah, so that's it!

Anyway, Barbara called me from her dad's house after the shopping trip. *

---

*She was there because they were going to leave for Boston the next day to attend the wedding of middle sister Gwen. I would be flying up a day later. In case you're interested, younger sister Karen had become officially engaged to Gary. The whole family was out at a restaurant and, when Karen went to the bathroom, Gary slipped the ring under her napkin. She came back, saw the ring, and said, "Oh," and emitted an embarrassed giggle, which I thought was an appropriate reaction considering the excitement Barb and I had elicited from the family with our announcement.

"We had so much fun. We bought little T-shirts, and little stretchy outfits, and caps, and an outfit to bring the baby home from the hospital, and blankets, and a gray-and-white quilt (to go with our living room), and, oooh, we even got this little stretchy outfit that looks like a baseball uniform. And you get a bunch of things for a girl and a bunch of things for a boy, and when the baby's born, you call them and pick up the right ones."

So that's what a layette is!

Eight Weeks to Go

We were in Boston, attending Gwen's wedding when Barbara matter-of-factly reminded me that the due date was eight weeks from that day.

I won't say I was surprised to hear that; the introductory packet we had received from the hospital the week before had been an indication that we were getting close. This packet had all kinds of useful information about visiting hours and types of rooms and so forth, as well as a zillion or so forms to fill out so we wouldn't have to fill them out while It was happening, at which time I would be as likely to try to smoke a pen as write with it.

Ah, but eight weeks. Just a few days earlier, somebody at the office had been telling me about a certain cousin of hers who had been two months premature. And that meant It could happen any day! And we hadn't even started breathing classes yet! What if tomorrow Barbara said, "It's time"? What would I do? When should I say "Push"? How would I fill out the forms?

Ooooh, boy!

Now I won't say that this pronouncement of eight weeks to go produced second thoughts on my part. Obviously it was too late for that. And not only because there was nothing I could do about the baby short of changing my name and moving somewhere with no extradition agreements. It was too late for second thoughts because I had already had third, fourth, fifth, and twenty-eighth thoughts.

With eight weeks to go, every reluctance I ever had about having a kid resurfaced like a bad Mexican dinner. Of course having all these thoughts now was like trying parachuting and remembering you're afraid of heights after you've jumped. There's nothing left to do but pull the ripcord.

I'm not sure if Barbara was sharing these thoughts. I do know, however, that as we sat at a table in a Boston restaurant, she looked at her stomach (which was getting pummeled from the inside) and said, "Stupid baby, stupid baby."

I know she really didn't mean it.

This May Sound Silly, But . . .

This may sound silly, but we were really getting attached to the little guy.

You can only have conversations with something for so long before you start attributing characteristics to it and giving it a personality.

We knew, for instance, that C.M. was up and wanting to be played with every night around eleven. Played with? Sure. We watched Barbara's stomach as it moved, then rubbed where we thought the baby was. Then the baby would move somewhere else, and we'd find it again. Prenatal hide-and-seek, if you will. One night I even tried to play catch with C.M. I rolled a ball over Barb's tummy, and we watched her stomach move after it like an ocean wave. Unfortunately C.M. refused to throw the ball back.

Barbara insisted that C.M. knew when we were going to visit grandfather Stanley and genuinely looked forward to the trips. She was also certain that C.M. was afraid of the dark and actually attempted to prove it.

"Look," she said one night when we were in bed, "see my stomach moving?"

"Yeah."

"Now watch." She took the blanket and covered her stomach. Then she put my hand on it. "See? It's not moving anymore."

"Barbara," I argued. "It's already dark in there. It doesn't make any difference if you're covered with a blanket."

"Why not? Skin is translucent."

"I think there's a couple of other layers between your skin and the baby." She pouted. I should have humored her.

It became even easier to treat C.M. like a human being as we began preparing for his/her arrival. Would C.M. like this crib? Would this stroller be good for C.M.'s back? Would C.M. enjoy this toy? We interviewed a pediatrician, so C.M. now had a doctor. And we watched TV shows about child development so we'd know what C.M. was *really* doing when he/she was doing whatever he/she would be doing. For instance, we knew just when C.M. would start sitting up straight and walking. (Interestingly these were two abilities that were presently fading fast in C.M.'s mother.)

Anyway I got to thinking one day that if anything should go wrong with the pregnancy or birth, we would really feel a deep loss. We already had a baby that we had grown to love. We had spent almost nine months watching our baby grow up to become a newborn.

The Psychology of Babies and Jobs

In early June, my boss took me out to lunch to give me a psychology lesson. He started with the fact that every person at our agency who had ever had a baby had left or tried to leave his or her job for a new one. "Do you know why that is?" he asked.

I figured it wasn't some obvious reason like wanting a lot more money. If it was, the whole conversation would have had an anticlimactic air to it.

He explained that when people have babies, they suddenly feel very locked into their personal lives. This makes them panic and look around frantically for anything left that is still changeable. Usually that is their job.

I was very uncomfortable as he spoke about this, not only because it was clearly intended to make a point about my present circumstances, but also because I had had a job interview that morning.

This other job seemed very attractive: There was more money involved, plus I would be the sole proprietor of the creative department instead of sharing those duties.

I had a lot more interviews and then, at the end of June, an offer. Barb and I had a decision to make.

Of course, I thought about what my boss had said. I decided I disagreed. If anything the coming baby made me reluctant to accept this new position. I felt that my personal life was about to be thrown into turmoil, and I wanted to stabilize whatever I could. Then there were the additional responsibilities. Would I be able to spend as much time as I wanted to with my new family?

Ultimately Barb pointed out that this was the type of position I'd always wanted and that if a new job were going to keep me away, we were better off having that happen in the first year than later on when the baby would know who I was. Of course the extra money would alleviate many of my fears about having a baby. We would definitely be able to keep our video club membership. And it made a two-bedroom apartment in Manhattan more within reach.

I took the job after making sure that maternity benefits would be covered and that my new employers wouldn't mind having a lunatic creative director for a month or so. Now I had to give notice to my boss, knowing that I would be adding fuel to his fire about babies.

He listened to all my reasons for leaving: money, position, control. He said it was funny about the way babies controlled your life so you longed to be in control of something else. I thought (but didn't say) that if control was the whole issue, I could have bought an ant farm and played god to insects.

I do agree with my old boss, however, that there probably is something deeply psychological about the desire to change jobs when a baby comes.

Still, the money doesn't hurt.

How to Give Birth (and Why It's Amazing We Even Managed to Conceive Without a Six-part Course)

THE FIRST CLASS

At the beginning of June, we started our childbirth course. It was something we had both been looking forward to because, as Barb put it, it was the first thing we were doing together as a family. It also signaled that we were coming down the homestretch and, frankly, we were both sick of Barbara's being pregnant.

The class was held across the street from the hospital in the un-air-conditioned apartment of Stacy, a jolly black woman with a delightful Caribbean accent. There were five other couples in the class, and I was happy to see that most of the other women had the good manners not to look any better than Barbara.

Stacy began by distributing some handouts: a two-page photocopied article and a glossy magazine. I'll get to those later. She also had everyone sign up for free magazines, which, she promised, would at the very least bring everybody a lot of store coupons.

When everyone was comfortable (in the case of a roomful of pregnant women, this can take an hour or two), Stacy dove right in, starting with the really important stuff like which door of the hospital we should enter through. This prompted the first question from the class: about the availability of parking facilities, the answer to which made me happy to know we'd be taking a cab.

"You can even drop her off at the emergency room," Stacy told the inquirer who seemed certain his child would be born at three in the morning. "I'll teach you how to time the contractions so you'll know how much time there is. In fact, when I get finished with you, you'll even be able to deliver." She laughed at this—a hearty West Indian laugh that made her sound something like a female Santa Claus. "I did have one daddy who had to catch the baby. The nurses said to me, 'Oh, that daddy was good. He was fantastic.'" I was ready to go home and oil my baseball glove.

Stacy told us the difference between labor rooms, delivery rooms, recovery rooms, and birthing rooms.

"The labor room is to labor in. You deliver in the delivery room." It sounded as though the rooms had been aptly named.

"In the birthing room you labor *and* deliver. Who makes the decision?" I had an idea, but she answered before I could raise my hand.

"Well, your doctor is part of it." Some doctors, it seemed, did not like the birthing room. Ours didn't mind it and, according to Stacy, would deliver the baby anywhere: "Inside out, upside down, just give him a little room, and he'll deliver you." This was good to know in case Barb went into labor while on an amusement park ride.

What was the big advantage of a birthing room? It had a TV. I figured I'd demand a birthing room if the baby was going to come during "Wheel of Fortune."

Stacy told us specifically which rooms to ask for and which to avoid. Rooms four and six had telephones and so were desirable. "Don't get number eight," she warned. "There's no windows, and it's so small, there's hardly room for a third person." I knew that if we got the horrible number eight, I would make the sacrifice and give up my space to the doctor, because I thought, hell, Barbara *had* to be there.

"Now the mommy will go into a room to get dressed and you have a decision to make." I was surprised at this, as I hadn't thought the hospital gave you a choice of what to wear, but Stacy continued: "The daddy can go into the dressing room with the mommy, or he can wait till she's ready. I personally think he should go in with her. Why?"

This question was asked with an emphasis to show it was rhetorical, which was good, because I didn't even know a good reason why I should be in the *delivery room,* much less the dressing room. (A month earlier, a cousin had asked if, considering how much I had been traveling on business, I intended to be home for the birth. I replied that if she meant home, as opposed to in the delivery room, the answer was yes. Barbara responded by kicking me in the shin.)

Stacy answered her own question: "Because otherwise you'll break the rhythm. I expect you to do some laboring at home, so by the time you get to the hospital, you'll be in good labor." Barbara winced at this; apparently she didn't anticipate it would be very good.

"You'll be breathing together and then Mommy goes into the dressing room, and you lose the rhythm, and what happens?" This was another rhetorical question. "Mommy panics."

"I *will* be panicked," Barb whispered to me.

"So will I," I whispered back.

"So Daddies," said Stacy, "go in with her. You can help her get undressed."

She then told us about all the women who were stupid enough to wear slacks. "Wear something loose. No need to get dressed up." This was good to hear; I knew Barb had picked out a gown for the occasion.

The next subject was the monitors that would get hooked up, one for contractions, the other for the baby's heartbeat.

"This monitor must have *contact*." She said this as though we would be responsible for the connection. "So they will put jelly on for *contact*." I was trying to figure out why the word *contact* was so important. I wondered whether, if one of us said it, a duck would come down from the ceiling.

"If it is on for awhile, the jelly dries out because you move, and guess what? No *contact*. And suddenly, there will be no heartbeat on the monitor. Don't panic. It's just because there's no *contact*."

This was absolutely important advice. If I hadn't heard it and the monitor stopped in the delivery room, I would've been climbing the doctor's back for explanations.

On to the topic I know I was anxious to hear about.

"Enemas. We only try to use enemas if it's early in labor. This cleans out the rectum so that when you push the baby out, you don't push out fecal matter, too."

Good idea, I thought. We wouldn't want the doctor reaching for the wrong thing.

"You don't want to have the enema too late, because you might have the baby in the toilet."

And then someone could say, "Gee, your baby looks flushed."

"Shaving." Stacy had this habit of formally introducing each subject.

"At this hospital, we generally don't do it." I was relieved to hear this, because in the panic of labor I might slit my throat trying to shave.

"Not even for C-sections. Now we do what we call a bikini cut." She went on about the whys and wherefores of C-sections.

After awhile it became apparent that just about everything that's done during labor is for the sole purpose of distracting the woman from her pain.

"That's one good reason to have the enema. You spend twenty minutes on the toilet and it distracts you from the pain." I thought that perhaps calling in a few male strippers would be a little less drastic a distraction than an enema. I remembered all the prison breakout movies I had seen: "Okay, Mumbles, you go around the back and give the guards enemas to create a diversion. We'll bust out of here while they're in the john."

"Intravenous." The next subject had been introduced.

"It's the policy of this hospital to give everyone an intravenous." I hoped this did not include fathers.

"That is unless it's very late in labor. Some people come in and the baby's head is already out. They have the babies in the elevator." This was not what I wanted to hear. My biggest fear besides having the baby look like one of my fat aunts was for Barbara to deliver the baby on the corner of Fourteenth Street and Sixth Avenue.

"This mostly happens with people having their second babies," Stacy said. I was, naturally, glad to hear this because I wanted to be sure to have something left to worry about when we had our next baby.

Stacy described precisely where to have the intravenous, a couple of inches above the wrist. This would allow for movement during delivery.

"Sometimes they have medical students do this. You have the right to refuse. If they don't get it the second try, definitely ask for someone else." No kidding!

Stacy wanted to be sure we knew how important it was for the daddies to participate. "When you participate, you are less nervous. It is the daddies who don't participate who faint." She informed us that our doctor even allowed the daddies to cut the umbilical cord. I thought that this might be taking participation a little too far; I'd be afraid of performing a bris by mistake.

Next Stacy used a flip chart to show us how the fetus develops. Barb and I had already seen most of this in our books and had been following along during the pregnancy. ("So this is what C.M. looks like now. Isn't it cute?") Then she turned on the TV and popped in a videocassette. At first a rerun of

"M＊A＊S＊H" came on, and I thought Alan Alda was going to deliver our baby. But then she clicked on the VCR, and we saw a brief film about childbirth, which included a bloody newborn being handed over to a father who appeared to be suffering from jaundice. I learned two things from this film:

1. Stacy's TV needed its color adjusted.

2. Somebody had damned well better wash off that baby before they tried to hand it to *me*.

During the film, Stacy laid exercise mats and pillows out on the floor and after she had turned off the TV and all the mommies had gone to the bathroom, we all took our positions on the mats like some sort of incredibly obese gymnastics team. The girls did some exercises, the men practiced massage, and then we learned how to breathe during labor.

"Don't be fooled by false labor," Stacy warned. "If the contractions come ten minutes then seven minutes then fifteen minutes, that's not labor. Just go back to sleep. If you can go back to sleep, you *really* know it's not labor. In labor the contractions get closer and longer. Ten minutes, ten minutes. Seven minutes, seven minutes. Like that." I hoped for Barbara's sake she was describing the length of time between contractions and not the duration of the contractions themselves.

Here's how to breathe during a contraction: two deep breaths at the beginning of each one, then rhythmic breathing during the contraction, then two deep breaths at the end.

"The baby will thank you for the two breaths at the end," Stacy told us. "You'll see on the monitor the heartbeat get fast. That's the baby thanking you for the oxygen. It's saying "Thank you, Mommy.""

It was up to the daddy to supply the beat for the rhythmic breathing. Barb and I had already anticipated that this would be a problem as rhythm is not exactly my strong point. In fact I don't even clap my hands in public because I never seem to be clapping along with everyone else. We considered bringing a metronome to the hospital.

Stacy sent us home to practice our breathing and ordered the daddies not to miss the next class. No way. I had too much to learn.

The next day I took the time to look through the literature Stacy had given us. First there was a two-page photocopied article called "The Last Eight Weeks of Pregnancy." This was, if you'll excuse the expression, a sort of crib sheet in case we missed any pertinent information in the class, and included a section called "The Essential Layette." It listed everything a layette should have (where was this thing when I needed to know what a layette was?) including "bunting." I always thought bunting was the red, white, and blue streamers stores hung outside for grand openings. What did this have to do with my baby? Were we supposed to hang it outside our apartment to announce the birth? I looked for an explanation. Next to *bunting* it said: "Nice to have for the outdoors. But wait, this is the present most people choose."

Well we'd already assigned all the furniture, so I guessed the next person who asked what we needed would be told "bunting." Then we'd just wait and see what showed up.

A major section of Stacy's handout was devoted to "What to Expect as Delivery Nears." The first two paragraphs in this section were called "Lightening" and "Show." I now knew that a severe storm followed by a cabaret act meant it was time to go to the hospital. Subsequent paragraphs were called "False Labor," "Rupture of the Membranes," "Timing Labor Pains," "The Three Stages of Labor," "At the Hospital," and "Delivery." This was all on a two-page handout, remember. It made me wonder why we were taking a six-part course to learn all this stuff.

The magazine Stacy had given us was called *Pre-parent Advisor, A Guide to Getting Ready for Birth 1985–1986.*

How, I wondered, had getting ready for birth been different in the 1983–1984 season? The magazine did not answer this question.

As it turned out, the publication's primary purpose was to carry advertising for Johnson & Johnson baby products, but it did have some interesting articles in it.

There was, for instance, the obligatory piece on baby naming: "There's been a swing from Tom, Dick and Harry to the more sophisticated Christopher, Matthew and Joshua," said the article. Terrific! We had thought up a sophisticated name for our child. Now, what about Casey? "Unisex names are increasingly popular for little girls . . ." Boy, did we do well!

The next article that caught my eye was entitled "Also Starring . . . Dad." Here are some choice excerpts:

> In the 1980s, when more than 80 percent of U.S. hospitals encourage husbands to be present in the delivery room, it's hard to believe that as recently as 15 years ago, a man's primary function was to deliver his wife safely to the hospital door and then prowl the waiting room or nearby taverns awaiting the good news.

Well, that may be progress, but, on the other hand, I had saved up nine months worth of *Newsweek* I had been planning to read in the waiting room.

> The expectant father may fret about the fact that his life will never be the same again and that he'll have to share his wife's interest, devotion, and even her body with the child.

That's okay. There was plenty of her to share.

> Swayed by her "nesting" instinct, your wife may be tirelessly organizing and scrubbing the house, but in preparing the baby's room, you should be the one who's painting, hammering, climbing ladders, and lugging furniture.

Yeah, well as far as that "nesting" instinct goes, the writer of this article obviously hadn't checked our floors.

> Attending childbirth classes together not only brings you closer as a couple but also gives the mother a much-needed psychological boost. Chances are that she's feeling vulnerable and unsure in these final weeks and needs a partner who is knowledgeable and in control, particularly if anything unexpected should happen.

I was more than happy to attend the classes with Barbara, but I wondered where she was going to find someone who was in control. If anything unexpected were to happen, she was going to have a tough time just reviving me from the Valium.

> Scratch a father who has just attended the birth of his child and you'll likely find a man in ecstasy, unashamedly calling the event "the most wonderful thing I've ever done."

I was sure it would be exciting, but there was this time about eight years earlier when I came up to bat with the bases loaded in the ninth inning with two out and my team down three runs and blasted this mammoth triple over the left fielder's head . . .

In a serious vein, there was one article in this magazine that managed, in a relatively small space, to hit upon every emotion I was experiencing. It was called "The Stress of Becoming a Father." I include it here in its brief entirety, in case your childbirth teacher doesn't give you this magazine, because reading these words will make you feel more normal in knowing every expectant father has the anxieties you're going through.

> Unsettling as the last trimester is for a mother-to-be, a father-to-be has his own struggles with impending

parenthood. While his wife is wondering about her abilities as a mother, he's wondering whether he's ready to be a father. She's experiencing emotional ups and downs; he's feeling confused and vulnerable.

A man expects a great deal of himself at this time. He expects to be a stoic individual, to support his family both financially and emotionally, and to be strong and reliable. Often, though, he's not quite sure he's up to the task.

According to Howard Osofsky, M.D., chief psychiatrist at the Menninger Foundation, men typically undergo considerable stress and upheaval during the course of a pregnancy. Following their initial excitement and pride, some husbands feel strange—not entirely themselves. They may become panicky and wonder whether or not they can handle the responsibilities a new baby entails. They might have trouble adjusting to the prospect of sharing their affections with a newcomer.

All these concerns make communication difficult at a time when spouses most need mutual support. Helping each other will be easier if each partner recognizes the emotional challenges the other must weather during this time of change and growth.

If there was one thing I came away with after reading all this material, it was a deeper appreciation of Barbara than I had ever had before. It wasn't just all the internal things she was dealing with, but also the way she was handling our relationship. The focus of many of the articles in this magazine was how fathers should be tolerant of how badly they were likely to be treated by their wives and how neglected they would feel.

I felt none of that. Throughout the pregnancy, Barbara had been loving, sharing, and supportive, even when the changes her body was going through must have seemed intolerable. I'm not sure what kind of impression you're getting of my wife from reading this book, but let me set you straight right now: No expectant father could be luckier than I.

The night I read the magazine, I came home with flowers.

THE SECOND CLASS

The second class took place on a sweltering June night and Stacy left the lights off in the apartment to keep it as cool as possible, which was not very cool. And what's not very cool to expectant fathers is *really* not very cool to expectant mothers.

It was hot!

After distributing more handouts, Stacy began by reviewing the flip chart and reminding us about the pelvis and the mucus plugs and the ruptured membranes.

"Labor. There's no way to know how long labor will be. Some people think you can tell by how long your mother was in labor. So ask your mother, and if she was only in labor an hour . . ." I wished Stacy would move on to another subject, as this could only be upsetting Barbara. I looked over to her; she seemed sad but in control.

"Of course," Stacy continued, "your mother may have had a short labor because in those days, they put the mommies to sleep. And what did we do with the daddies? We put them in the waiting room." Stacy sounded incredulous, but, damn it, it still didn't seem like such a bad idea.

We learned that one of the important preparatory steps was to be sure the daddies knew where the doctor's phone number was. "You start labor," said Stacy, "and your brain seems to go on vacation. Daddy says, 'where's the number' and you just go 'uh, uh.' Make sure Daddy knows where the number is."

"Women in labor are very vulnerable," Stacy told us. "You say, 'Oh, no, she is strong.' But she's a totally different person in labor." If that was true, I hoped she'd be a rich person.

On to the next subject: "Nutrition. Protein is helpful. Eat

eggs, chicken, turkey. You digest chicken and turkey better than beef. And liver. Liver is very good." This produced a chorus of groans from the class.

"Some doctors give you an iron supplement. They can give you constipation or diarrhea." Well that pretty well covered the possibilities.

"Feel free to ask the doctor for another kind." ("Uh, doctor, this supplement gives me diarrhea. Can I please have the one that gives me constipation?")

"If you are a smoker, cut down. At the onset of labor, stop completely. They have done research in England that shows the baby gets much more oxygen if you don't smoke through labor. If Daddy smokes"—she cleared her throat to show her disapproval—"he is to smoke by the window." Barbara elbowed me. She must have known I was still grubbing at the office.

"Alcohol. When they speak of alcohol in pregnancy, they are talking about someone who is an alcoholic and not eating. But if you go out for dinner and have an occasional glass of wine, they are not making a big deal out of it." Stacy made it sound like if you had more than one glass, they'd send the pregnancy police out after you.

Stacy then discussed back labor. It was the coach's (that was me) job to massage the small of the back with his fist if there was a back labor, which is when the back of the baby's head is toward the mother's back.

"How will you know it's back labor?" Stacy asked. "The mother will say, 'Ooooh, my back, my back!'" I somehow thought that what Barbara would say would be somewhat less intelligible and would involve a lot of frantic pointing.

"Never leave her flat on her back. Big no-no." Well that's how I got into this mess in the first place.

Somewhere during her speech, Stacy got to talking about other people's babies and how we shouldn't try to deliver them. "You can give instructions, but these days, blood is a fluid you don't want to come into contact with." I know one of the things the class was supposed to do was give us confidence, but I doubted I'd want to go wandering around the hospital while Barb was in labor to see if there were any other deliveries I could help out with. I could just see Barb having to hold me back: "No, no, I know how much you love delivering babies, but you might get AIDS or something. Well, okay, if you must, but don't touch the blood." Yeah, suuuuuurrrrre!

Stacy, meanwhile, already had our baby out of the womb. "The baby's out, the first thing Mommy wants it on her stomach." That way, it could kick the outside for awhile.

Stacy explained that first the doctor would make sure the umbilical cord wasn't around the neck, and then would check for good muscle tone, which indicates that the baby is ready to breathe. Next, the baby gets suctioned out, which sets him or her to screaming. Finally the baby is set on the mother's stomach with the cord still attached. "But some babies have short cords," Stacy said. "Then the mommy can't have it on her abdomen."

"Can't you get an extension cord?" I asked, only because the straight line was too good to resist. This drove Stacy to riotous laughter while the rest of the class giggled uncomfortably. I decided they were taking this whole thing much too seriously. Come on, kids, have some fun with it!

I know what you're thinking. You're thinking I was making light of the classes, of the baby, of the pregnancy, of the birth. Well you're wrong. I wanted to learn all I could to make everything go smoother. But I was going to have a good time doing it. I wanted to enjoy the pregnancy and the birth because I still wasn't sure I'd exactly have a ball *after* the birth. Besides, somebody had to be the class clown!

Stacy went into a discussion of toxemia, blood pressure, and so on, and then it was time for the evening's film, which I was looking forward to because the topic had already been announced as breast-feeding.

What a disappointment!

Not that I'm particularly sexist, but I enjoy looking at a

good breast like anyone else. Well, let me tell you, nothing ruins the pure pornographic value of bare boobs like attaching babies to them. Plus this movie featured women that were so ugly, I couldn't help wondering if extreme unattractiveness was a side effect of breast-feeding. I worried that after six months or so of nursing, Barbara's nose would grow and she'd suddenly want to wear pointy eyeglasses from the fifties and put her hair up in a bun.

The exercises in the second class posed a problem. First we played role reversal, and the daddies had to breathe like we were going through the last stages of labor so we'd get an idea of what our wives would go through. This is very quick, shallow breathing, the kind that makes me cough. I coughed. It ruined the rhythm.

Then we practiced coaching our wives through the various stages of labor. Barb and I had practiced the first stage and had found that I could just about keep the rhythm by yelling "IN" at three-second intervals as timed by my digital watch. By the time we got to the last stage, I was up to one-second intervals, which tended to sound like "ININININININININININ-ININININININ." I managed to keep that going for about ten seconds before tripping on my tongue. To further complicate matters, Stacy kept calling out various parts of Barb's anatomy that were hypothetically experiencing cramps so I could massage them. Now I had to massage, look at my watch, and emit a continuous stream of "INs" (which was beginning to sound like a Hindu chant) simultaneously. This constituted an incredible feat of coordination. I could only hope that Barbara would be able to get me through labor.

This time there were three pieces of literature, which I dutifully read the next day. The first was a typewritten, two-page document entitled "Touch Relaxation." The first page was a list of all massaging techniques for every part of Barbara's body that could conceivably tense up during labor. For instance:

She presses upper legs together as if to hold a sheet of paper between them. Touch — start high on inside thigh and stroke firmly down to knee, lightly up on the outside, and begin again. Useful in transition if legs begin to shake.

Well, this was all right, providing I could get enough leverage to stroke firmly while *my* legs were shaking. But there were eleven different techniques on the first page and then, on the second page, there was a list of all the things the coach was supposed to do during the stages of labor. Look at all the things I had to take care of just during the 3–7 centimeter stage:

Call out apex, end of contractions
Remind her to relax
Provide quiet atmosphere — low lights, door closed
Remind her to urinate
Use effleurage if helpful
Give ice chips, washcloth to face and body
Back rub/counterpressure with back labor
Offer socks if feet are cold
Remind her of progress

There was a similar list for the three other stages; I counted twenty-three different chores. Plus the eleven massage techniques. Plus timing the contractions and keeping the rhythm. It was beginning to appear that one of the goals of this whole coaching thing was to make childbirth as mentally painful for the father as it was physically painful for the mother. I mean I hadn't had to remember so many things since I'd crammed for a high school chemistry test. Geez, Barb didn't have to remember to do anything; all she had to do was be in agony.

I just wasn't going to remember all this stuff unless I took the list to the hospital, and I couldn't see how I was going to be able to consult the list while I was looking at my watch and keeping time.

I wondered if I could bring an assistant.

The second piece of literature was a pamphlet from the March of Dimes called "Recipe for Healthy Babies," a guide to nutrition. And a very helpful one at that. I kid you not, this was really the first sentence of text: "Food is nutritious only when it's eaten."

This was very distressing to hear, since for nine months I had been smearing food on Barbara's abdomen so the nourishment could go right to baby. I decided not to read the rest of that pamphlet in case there were other great tips like always taking the shells off the eggs before you eat them.

Finally there was a small magazine called *Expecting*. It was published by *Parents* magazine, in the hopes of getting new parents to subscribe to their publication. The first article that caught my eye was "Parents Talk about Labor," which was subtitled "And Why You Should Expect the Unexpected." It was the lead-in blurb that got my attention:

> Your fantasy of what labor will be like probably has
> been formed from many sources: books, conversations
> with friends . . .

Call me crazy, but my fantasies tend toward thoughts of joining several women in doing things that are illegal in many states or making incredible catches in the seventh game of the World Series. Of course I am a man, but I'm sure no woman fantasizes about labor either unless she is a closet masochist. Barbara was worried about labor, yes, but she did not fantasize about it. She did fantasize, as I did, about the baby itself—holding it, cooing at it, and watching it grow up to be terribly successful and support its parents in their old age—but it seemed to me that fantasizing about labor is no more likely than having wet dreams about brussels sprouts.

There was one more terrific article in this magazine. It was called "Sing to Your Baby!" Get a load of this first paragraph:

> Along the Northwest coast, native Americans believed
> that a baby had to be kept happy or he would get

discouraged and die. To prevent this, mothers and fathers sang special songs to their infants, encouraging them to grow and become adults. A father would sing to his son about the duties and privileges he would someday have as a hunter or fisherman. A mother would sing to her daughter, imagining the day when she would pick berries or sew a deerskin dress. This Indian folklore may be closer to the truth than we realize.

Okay, how's this: "Oh, son of mine in New York City / Such a wealthy surgeon you could be. / Better yet, your parents will be thanking / You to study corporate banking."

Of course it was possible that our baby would thrive on such songs. Babies do not have much in the way of musical taste. On the other hand, I was quite sure our neighbors (and the parent who wasn't singing) would *not* thrive and might even sue.

THE HOSPITAL TOUR

When you're in New York, you take a museum tour. When you're in Los Angeles, you take a tour of the stars' homes. When you're in your eighth month of pregnancy, you take a tour of a maternity ward.

And so, on a warm Sunday in June, Stacy led the class through the corridors of Beth Israel Hospital.

The class assembled in the hospital's admitting room, which gave the attending staff quite a start. Not working in maternity, they were not expecting a bunch of near-end-of-term preggos to show up and make themselves comfortable. They seemed relieved when Stacy arrived and led us away.

We were shown the entrance we should use, an ambulance ramp that was next to the emergency room but allowed us to circumnavigate it, since, Stacy said, that facility was bound to be filled with winos who had evidently discovered that if they stayed long enough, they'd get a free meal (but then it *was* hospital food). This ramp was fairly steep, and there was some talk of the husbands chipping in to buy a hand truck to get our wives to the entrance.

We were instructed to ignore the emergency room entirely and go directly into an elevator and up to the fourth floor. Here we were given yellow gowns that went on backward and tied behind you, in order, I could only guess, to make it as difficult as possible to get and keep the thing on by yourself. It occurred to me that it would be a good idea to abscond with a dozen or so of these outfits so Barbara could wear them during meals to protect her clothes. This latest in disposable attire came with matching elasticized caps and shoe covers. When we were finished dressing, we looked like a bunch of bananas about to take showers.

Stacy showed us the room board, where you could see which rooms were available. She showed us the desirable number six and the dreaded number eight. We saw how the beds and monitors worked. She showed us where the all-important ice machine was (the daddies were to keep the mommies' lips moist with ice chips) and let us taste the alternative—a sort of Q-tip soaked in glycerin.

Stacy then had the daddies put on masks that made us look like a bunch of bananas that were about to take a shower and then go rob a bank. The gowns were already hot; the masks also made it difficult to breathe. I wondered why the girls didn't need the masks for the next part of the tour. Were they more sterile than us? "No," said Stacy, "I just want the daddies to get used to the masks. You may have to wear them awhile."

We saw the delivery room, with surprisingly narrow tables, stirrups, and huge spotlights (and it was obvious what they were pointed at). A nearby operating room for C-sections was similar. The class, I think, was now hot and bored.

We wanted to see babies!

We entered the intensive care department where problem babies, mostly premature infants, were kept. Through windows we saw the tiny things, some about the length of my sneaker. Many of them were in clear boxes, hooked up to all sorts of things. One—just one—cried.

Then it was upstairs to the main nurseries where we saw lots of babies—all born that weekend. They were really churning them out! There were Asian babies, white babies, and black babies. There were bald babies and babies with more hair than I have. There were small babies and a couple of nine-pound monsters. They were all asleep.

Stacy showed us all the various kinds of rooms we could opt for: semishared, semiprivate (shared bathroom), private, and private deluxe. This last cost $185 extra and included a sofabed, refrigerator, and 19-inch color TV, plus the daddy got free meals so he could eat with the mommy (but it *was* hospital food).

All in all the tour was pretty dull (except for the two families—one Hasidic, the other Chinese—we kept running into because they were wandering around looking for their newest relative). We all departed, heeding Stacy's warning to remember to remove the hospital garments before taking to the street. (They *would* look strange even in Greenwich Village.)

Now I knew that the main purpose of the classes and the hospital tour was so that we'd be prepared for everything that was going to happen and would know precisely what to do. So far I definitely knew one thing: When everything that was going to happen was happening, there had better be a nurse around to tell us precisely what to do.

THE THIRD CLASS

June was a very nice month weatherwise. Pretty cool, breezy—perfect spring weather. Except Mondays. Mondays were hot. And Stacy's apartment still wasn't air-conditioned.

The night of the third class felt even hotter, mostly because the class was comparatively uninteresting. Lots of real technical stuff about presentation, cervical effacement, and levels of descent.* There was even a slide show instead of the usual film, with chintzy illustrations depicting, among other things, how to push properly.

We then took to the mats to practice this. The daddies sit behind the mommies, with Mommy's head more or less in Daddy's lap. At the start of a contraction, there's the deep cleansing breath — in and out — then a second breath that gets held while Daddy counts to fifteen Mississippi. In the meantime, Mommy brings her knees up as far as they will go (which isn't very) and holds them up by putting her hands under her thighs, elbows out. (I'm sure this is necessary for pushing, but from my perspective during the class, the appearance of five pregnant women lying on the floor with their knees in the air and their elbows extended brought to mind a school of shellfish.) Of course, we didn't actually practice pushing in class. It may have caused a half dozen premature deliveries or, worse, a flatulation chorus.

Even the handout, a second issue of *Expecting,* was dull. There was only one article that was even remotely interesting. It was called "Welcome to Parenthood," and it was about what to expect from your emotions and your baby in the first months. Choice excerpts follow, like the first sentences:

> Your baby is born. Friends and relatives are constantly calling to congratulate you or dropping by to ooh and aah and fuss over the baby.

Clearly the writers of this article hadn't met Barbara's family.

> Feeling that your baby has irrevocably changed your lives, and not necessarily for the better, creates a sense

---

*Presentation is how the baby's lying in the womb. Our doctor said he thought our baby was lying all right, which is to say, upside down. There should be something funny to say about that, but I can't think of anything. The levels of descent are measured by how low the baby is in the pelvis, and the unit of measurement is called a station. Therefore, the baby's level of descent could be, for instance, "station minus five." I thought this made the emerging of a baby sound too much like the landing of a space ship.

of guilt. You chose to bring a child into the world; she's
so innocent, so trusting, so beautiful, and you're un-
happy because you can't sleep late on Sunday morning? How trivial! How immature! Maybe you weren't
ready to have a child. Maybe you should have waited
a few more years. Maybe you're not equal to the re-
sponsibility of parenting.

Maybe the ninth month of pregnancy is the wrong time to
be reading this article. I stopped reading it.

I think even Stacy knew the class was dull; on the way out,
she promised more excitement for the next week: a film showing the actual birth. I told her I'd bring the popcorn.

THE FOURTH CLASS

It was immediately evident that the fourth class would be more
exciting than the third. Stacy began by distributing coupons
for Sheer Energy support pantyhose. This gave Barbara the
chance to enthrall the class with a bit of inside information:
L'eggs pantyhose sells what they call "Slightly Imperfects" by
mail order at about 50 percent of retail. What most people
don't know is that most of this hosiery isn't imperfect at all;
L'eggs just calls it that so the stores won't get angry that L'eggs
is undercutting them. Yes, folks, junk mail is a fascinating
business.

After the stocking discussion it was time for show and tell.
From a Rubbermaid container, Stacy started producing all
kinds of reproductive artifacts. First there was a sonogram
picture. "If you have a sonogram now," Stacy said, "they can
tell the sex. So you have to tell them if you don't want to know.
Because they get all excited and say 'It's a—'"

I've always thought this business of not wanting to know
the sex of the baby was a dumb tradition. All through our
pregnancy, people always asked if we knew the baby's sex.
Well we didn't, but I would have liked to. Why not? What's
the origin of the "I don't want to know" superstition? I don't

need the grand surprise. It would be enough of a surprise if I got through the delivery without passing out.

Next Stacy showed us a chart that told us what we were supposed to do at different points during the pregnancy. She looked around the class and said, "You're all about thirty-six weeks." Then she looked at Barbara and said, "Ooh, you look more than thirty-six weeks." This was not what I wanted to hear.

According to the chart, we were now supposed to pack our bag for the hospital. We were also supposed to stop having sex. We didn't need the chart to tell us that. At that point, if we'd wanted to have sex, we'd have needed instructions.

Other things started to pop out of Stacy's box. There was a 3-D chart that detailed the various stages of dilatation—from an opening about the size of a dime to something resembling a small frisbee. Then there was the tube they use if you need internal monitoring. This doesn't look like much at all unless, I guess, it's connected to something.

"If you hear 'ting ting' in the delivery room," said Stacy, "that's the internal monitor. If you hear 'thump thump' that's the external monitor." If we heard "bang bang," that would be me fainting and falling to the floor.

Stacy showed us an item that looked like a plastic crochet hook that the doctor uses to rupture the membrane. "If it ruptures at night and you're in bed, it'll wash the whole place away," she said. I hoped the crochet hook wouldn't be necessary; I was looking forward to having a tidal wave in our apartment.

The next accessory was an ordinary paper bag. "What is this for?" Stacy asked.

"For the father to throw up in?" I guessed.

This got a chuckle from the class, which was beginning to loosen up a bit. "No, no," said Stacy. "It's for hyperventilation."

Next was a page from a hospital equipment catalog that

depicted a bed called "The Maxima 200," which, the ad promised, "can handle all your delivery and gynecological surgical requirements." It looked like a fancy version of those contour beds they advertise on TV. I wondered if they made a queen-sized version.

"Now, daddies," said Stacy, holding up another chart, "this is in case you have to catch the baby. Just do the minimum. Use your shirt to wipe the baby off. Then hold it upside down and remove the mucus . . ." She pantomimed a massaging motion on a baby's neck. "Then put the baby on the mommy's breast—whether or not she's breast-feeding. This causes the uterine muscles to contract." As far as I was concerned, "the mimimum" would be calling 911 and then looking through my closet for a shirt it would be okay to ruin.

The final item in Stacy's collection was a purple and white woolen bag. I had noticed it earlier and had been curious about where it would come into the lecture. Stacy explained: "One of my clients—her seventy-nine-year-old mother knitted her uterus." This was getting absolutely bizarre. I mean talk about your weird hobbies. I had to have a talk with my mother; all she had knitted was a sweater. But wait, it gets better. By manipulating two sets of silver strings at the mouth of the sack, Stacy demonstrated dilatation. And then—there was the baby—a bright red whiffle ball! I was flabbergasted!

Now it was time for the movie. This incredible production was obviously produced during the sixties because everyone had long hair and there was a folk music sound track with an original song entitled "The Best Way to Show Your Love is to Be There." I wasn't sure, viewing the film, whether "be there" referred to the father or the cameraman.

The plot began in the delivery room with Mommy giggling during early labor and generally mugging for the camera. Daddy, who was wearing a yellow gown, cap, and mask (apparently delivery room fashions had not changed in two decades), was just wonderfully supportive. Then hard labor started and Mommy worked very hard and Daddy was *very* supportive. He was also now wearing a T-shirt that said COACH. The camera moved in for a close-up, which, if this were a porno movie, would be called explicit. The bearded doctor, who was wearing a T-shirt that said BABY CATCHER, shouted instructions. Finally, this greasy, red thing slid out along with some blood and other miscellaneous glop. As they wiped off the baby and suctioned its mouth, the placenta—a big, purplish sac—came out. Then the baby was put on its mother's breast and everyone posed for a picture as the theme song built to a big finish. One of the men in our class thought the baby had probably been named Moon Unit or something sixties like that.

The graphic detail of this movie was not only *not* conducive to the fathers being in the delivery room, it wasn't even conducive to the mothers being there.* But I did think the T-shirts were a good idea, in case anybody forgot who they were in the panic of the delivery room.

On the floor mats, we learned three new pushing positions. In the first position the moms were on their sides, one leg in the air, like a cocker spaniel that had somehow approached a fire hydrant horizontally. In the second position the mothers were on all fours with their weight shifted backward. They looked like a bunch of pit bull terriers about to engage in battle. The final position was the squat, which was too uncomfortable and acrobatic for any of the mothers to try for very long. It should be pointed out here, however, that in the ninth month of pregnancy just getting up out of a chair is an acrobatic feat of Olympian proportions.

---

*My mother, meanwhile, was determined to be at the hospital before, during, and after labor, even though we had politely told her that there was really no room or job for her other than to visit after the fact. Nevertheless she had called the hospital herself for directions and parking information, which meant, I can only imagine, that she expected that Barb and I would intentionally give her the wrong directions to throw her off the track. Maybe she thought we would direct her to St. Vincent's as a prank and laugh gleefully as she tried to find her way among the nuns.

Lots of handouts this time, but most were photocopied sheets with information and instructions that repeated stuff we had learned in class. I dutifully looked at it all anyway. One of the sheets was from Beth Israel and detailed the hospital's "rooming-in" option whereby the baby spends most of its time in the room with Mom instead of in the nursery. We had already decided against this, figuring the baby would, in short order, be spending just about *all* of its time with Mom and that Mom could use a day or two of vacation before taking the baby home.

THE FIFTH CLASS

The last class took place on the hottest day of the summer, temperature and humidity both topping out at around ninety-eight. It was the kind of day when everybody has those dark, wet, ugly stains under their arms—even if they're wearing sleeveless tops.

To make matters worse, my bursitis-stricken right elbow, which periodically fills with fluid, had decided that now was as good a time as any, and ballooned to the point where it looked like my upper and lower arm were connected by my chin.

Of course, the Second Avenue bus wasn't air-conditioned, but I did, mercifully, find a seat—next to a woman who spent the entire thirty-eight-block ride reading Deuteronomy in the Bible and underlining her favorite parts. Before boarding the bus this woman had bathed in a disgustingly sweet rose perfume. By the time I emerged from the bus on Fourteenth Street, I was sweaty and smelly. I felt like I'd just played a full court basketball game against a team of florists.

This was the condition I was in when my elbow and I met Barbara at Stacy's not-wired-for-air-conditioning apartment. But as hot as it was, it soon felt like Christmas, because Stacy had all kinds of presents for us: two prepackaged bags of *tchatchkes* from various advertisers, plus a truckload of reading material. Then she brought out the Rubbermaid basket again and showed us all sorts of new things.

It became uncomfortably noticeable that two couples were missing from the class. With all the women due about the same time and this being the last class, the absence of these couples was like a prisoner on death row not showing up for breakfast. Stacy told us one of them had called in sick, but then . . .

She began taking stuff out of the basket. First there were diapers: old-style disposables, new disposables (with resealable tape and gathers at the legs), newborn disposables, fourteen-pounds-and-up disposables, premature disposables, and finally cloth.

"Even if you are going to use disposables, buy at least a dozen cloth," Stacy instructed. Barb and I had already decided on the disposables even though the diaper services were cheaper. It just didn't make sense to keep a pailful of dirty diapers in a one-bedroom apartment, unless it was a different one-bedroom apartment from the one we were living in.

"Ah, but the cloth ones have other uses anyway," Stacy said, and demonstrated how you could drape one over your shoulder when burping the baby or put one under the baby in the crib to prevent spittle from getting on the sheets. I noticed that on days when the baby was particularly frustrating, these cloth diapers would make excellent surrender flags for Mommy and Daddy.

After telling us to buy at least six summer blankets, Stacy produced a large baby doll to demonstrate how to hold the baby. The recommended procedure was called the football hold, wherein the baby is tucked under your arm with his or her head in your hand. Stacy handed me the doll and I tried it. Sure enough, it was a comfortably snug position, even if I didn't exactly feel like Gale Sayers. I threw a pass to the daddy on the other end of the room so he could try it.

Next Stacy showed us three burping positions: on the lap, sitting up and leaning over your hand, and of course that old standby, over the shoulder. I tried it with the doll, and although I didn't hear a burp, it didn't drool all over me either.

Stacy showed us how to bathe our babies and how to administer CPR in case we drowned our babies.

One of the mommies asked how many pounds the doll would be if it were a baby. Stacy replied that it was a bit more than newborn, about twelve pounds. Then this mommy went on to talk about a baby she knows that gained five pounds in its first eight weeks, which didn't seem like a lot to me, as I've put on five pounds during one meal. Stacy "tsk-tsked" this obese baby.

"That is no good, " she said. "You know what will happen? Fatty cells." Aha! I knew my weight problem was my parents' fault!

As long as we were on the subject of eating, Stacy took from her basket all the different kinds of packaging in which formula could be purchased. If you like instant coffee, you'll love the powdered formula: Just add water, stir, pour into a bottle, and feed. If you like Campbell's soups, feed your baby the concentrated formula: Just water down the concentrate and feed. If you like frozen dinners, there's the ready-to-eat formula: Pour from can to bottle and you're all set. If you cook your frozen dinner in a microwave, buy the ready-to-eat that comes in its own bottle: Just pop on a nipple and serve. And finally, if you just order in Chinese, there's the ready-to-eat that comes in its own bottle with its own nipple. All you have to do is take the cover off and stick it in the kid's mouth.

Of course Stacy assumed that the mommies in our class would at least try breast-feeding.

"Those of you who are breast-feeding, I want you to take off your bras for a half hour or an hour every day and let the nipples rub against your clothes to toughen them up." In Barb's case, if it weren't for her stomach, they would rub against her knees.

"In Third World countries, they don't do any preparation of the breasts. But remember, in many of these countries, they go around topless." I vowed privately to see my travel agent immediately.

"If you get sore, you can use these." She showed us a box of Breast-eze, which were sort of screw-on nipples for breasts. Then she showed us catalog pages advertising all sorts of breast pumps: hand operated, battery powered, even electronic. I could just see Barbara at home and not able to answer the phone because her breasts were plugged in.

Next was my favorite item, a chart showing nine stool specimens.

"I want you to look at number nine very carefully," Stacy ordered. "That is diarrhea." I committed it to memory.

"Newborns can get diarrhea very easily. Call your doctor right away, because they can become dehydrated in twenty-four hours." Dehydration, she told us, was often prevented by feeding the baby a formula that was sort of an infant Gator-ade. Looking at the chart, I noticed that specimens two and three, black, mudlike stuff, were particularly disgusting. As we would see in that evening's movie, this stool had the additional attractive feature of being extremely plentiful and spreading all over the bottom half of the baby. Fortunately, Stacy said, this is a very early stool that is mostly all the prenatal stuff making its final exit, and it didn't usually last more than two days. In other words, the nurses in the hospital would be taking care of it. Yucch!

And then the phone rang.

The class was dead silent as we listened to Stacy's end of the conversation: "No pain? Three centimeters? Very nice." Sure enough, couple number five had gone into labor.

The movie showed adorable babies being held, fed, burped, bathed, and swaddled. That's about the extent of what you can do with a baby. They're not very versatile.

After the film Stacy thankfully announced that there would be no exercises that night, which was good since we probably would have adhered permanently to the mats. Instead there was an hour's worth of pep talk, final instructions, and questions.

Interestingly, I thought, all the mommies and daddies seemed reluctant to have the class end. It was as though leaving Stacy's apartment that night was the equivalent of having somebody say, "Ha, ha, you're on your own now, my lovelies." Yes, we all had a working knowledge of what would happen. But nobody seemed quite ready to cut the umbilical cord with Stacy.

Nevertheless we did.

As soon as we arrived home, Barb and I opened our presents. The first was called Gift Pax and came in a blue plastic bag with little illustrations of babies on it. It contained a box of three Pampers and another box of three Luvs so that we could conduct a side-by-side waste test. There was also a packet of Lipton Instant Cinnamon Apple Herbal Tea, but it wasn't clear if this was for the baby or Barb. And then there was all this:

1. A pamphlet entitled "How to Give Your Baby a Clean, Comfortable Start in Life." This turned out to be an ad for Dreft detergent and included a 30¢ coupon.

2. An offer of a free gift from *Parents* magazine. The free gift, or course, was a free issue when you subscribed.

3. Two coupons from Evenflo—75¢ off a deluxe breast pump and 25¢ off nursing pads.

4. A mail-order offer that gave us the opportunity to obtain the Healthcheck digital thermometer, an $11.95 retail value, for only $7.00 plus 50¢ handling charge.

5. A coupon for $1.00 off on Pampers.

6. A pamphlet called "New Parents' Guide to Baby's Laundry." This began with "We believe baby's laundry is as special as baby is . . ." and turned out to be a thinly disguised ad for Ivory Snow. It included a 65¢ coupon, which meant that Ivory was perfectly willing to outbid Dreft for our patronage.

7. Another pamphlet warning against the use of chlorine bleach and offering a quarter off on unchlorinated Snowy bleach.

8. A mail-in offer to have film developed in Greensburg, Pennsylvania for just 5¢ a print.

9. A catalog from Pampers called "Softouches" that showed us all the neat things you could get with the "Bonus Bears" that appeared on Pampers boxes. These items included everything from "Pampers' Exclusive Designer Shirts," to "Pampers' Designer Bib Set," various toys and baby implements, and a Basic Protection Kit that I wanted to get because it included those infamous outlet plugs that I knew no relative would buy us. The catalog even came with twelve Bonus Bears to get us started.

Our other presents included a delightful board that we could mount on the wall near the telephone and on which we could write erasable instructions to babysitters with the pen that Velcroed onto it. There was also the inevitable naming book, which Barbara grabbed before I could hide but which, fortunately, reinforced our decisions. (Casey meant "brave" while Matthew meant "gift of the Lord.") There was a booklet with even more coupons and a book entitled "Delivery & Beyond," which covered everything we needed to know in fifty pages. I decided not to read it; it could only confuse me.

The next day, while I was sitting in my doctor's waiting room waiting for him to drain my elbow, I looked through the rest of the literature Stacy had given us. There was a card with a poem on one side and an ad for Similac formula on the other. The poem was apparently written by someone whose work is mostly published by Hallmark. There was a guide to feeding the baby that offered two options for preparing formula: the terminal heating method and the aseptic method. I knew I didn't want my baby involved with anything that used the word *terminal*.

There was a book on safety measures that told us all the wonderful things that could happen to baby. It seemed as though babies were experts at falling out of things, getting their heads, arms, and legs caught in things, bashing themselves on things, and poisoning themselves. How in the world would we be able to protect someone with such pronounced suicidal tendencies?

The final piece of literature was a magazine: *New Parent Advisor: A Guide to Life with a New Baby, 1986–1987.* I was happy that the advice in this publication, unlike that contained in the *Pre-parent Advisor,* would be valid into next year.

I leafed through the pages and felt I really couldn't deal with it. I warn you, during the ninth month of pregnancy you will experience information overload, that uncomfortable feeling you get when your mind balks at even one more piece of data: "NO MORE, NO MORE! I SWEAR, IF YOU ASK ME TO READ THAT ARTICLE ON DIFFERENT KINDS OF CRYING, I'LL FORGET THE THREE STAGES OF LABOR!" I vowed to put the magazine aside until after the birth, when I could forget all the prenatal information.

And then I took a deep breath. It was July 8, less than three weeks to go. *If* Barb was on schedule. But of course It could happen—gulp—any day.

Any day!

Little Stuff to Do and Think About While Tearing Your Hair Out Waiting

Thankfully, most of the shopping was done without me. The crib, dressing table, and layette had already been purchased with a minimum of decision making.

The stroller, however, was another matter. Karen and Barb had already made a few trips and had narrowed it down to the Japanese Aprica and the British Maclaren. This was not as narrow as it may seem, since the Aprica came in more models than General Motors produces (and, it seemed, in the same price ranges). I thought that $250 was a bit on the expensive side for a stripped-down stroller, without air-conditioning, stereo, sunroof, or automatic transmission. I think Karen thought this was expensive, too (remember, the stroller contract had gone to her and Gwen).

Finally Barbara dragged me to a discount house on Long Island where all the models were on display. We examined an Aprica and a Maclaren that converted into carriages.

"What's the difference?" I asked a salesperson.

"The Aprica's handle reverses," he replied. He demonstrated a mechanism by which the baby could be propelled backward instead of forward.

"So?" I said.

He looked at me like I was particularly dense. "Some people," he said with a note of indignation, "like to face their babies occasionally."

"What's the sticker price?"

"$249."

I figured the baby would feel better seeing where he or she was going.

Ultimately we decided on the Maclaren, not because it was cheaper, but because it was lighter and folded more easily. But also it was cheaper.

As we had been instructed, we packed an overnight bag a month before the due date. Here is what was crammed into the little suitcase:

1. One pair of quilted, fake-fur-lined slippers because Mommy's feet can get cold in the delivery room. Of course, if either Mommy or Daddy had gotten cold feet nine months earlier, we wouldn't have to be packing an overnight bag now.

2. One leather change purse filled with dimes and nickels to

use for phone calls. Quarters would have been easier, but we use all our quarters for the washing machine.

3. One tube Vaseline Lip Therapy, to keep Mommy's lips from cracking.

4. One blue rubber racquetball ball, to help massage the small of Barbara's back in case of back labor.

5. One portable stereo AM/FM/cassette player with headphones, so that Mommy would have something to listen and dance to during labor.

6. Two paper bags for hyperventilation. One for each of us.

7. Three nightgowns.

8. One bathrobe.

9. One washcloth, with which I would constantly wipe her sweaty brow.

10. Three paperbacks.

11. One travel alarm clock, so Barbara would know what time it was. I didn't think this was necessary. Before the birth it would be time to panic. After the birth it would be time to call everybody.

12. Barbara's kit bag that she always travels with. It contains shampoo, toothbrush and paste, deodorant—all that stuff—plus a sewing kit. I didn't even want to think about possible uses of this last item on our upcoming trip.

13. One nursing bra.

14. One microcassette recorder with which I intended, much to Barbara's chagrin, to record the entire proceedings.

15. Four microcassettes in case it was a long night.

16. Two extra sets of batteries for the stereo and the micro.

17. Ten prerecorded cassettes. What's good delivery room music, you ask? Here's what Barb packed: The Roches, The Bangles, The Alan Parsons Project, Phil Collins, Sting, Alan Parsons again, The Manhattan Transfer, the soundtrack of "Girl Groups: The Story of a Sound," Tracey Ullman, and Whitney Houston. I'm sure all the people on this list are duly honored.

18. One pair of socks.

19. One hairbrush.

20. One makeup case so the baby could see Barb at her best.

21. One jar of Vaseline for Barbara's lips.

22. One camera, loaded with 400 ASA film to take lowlight pictures.

23. Seven candy bars: five Cadbury Fruit & Nut, one Baby Ruth, one Heath Bar. When I went through the suitcase to write this section, I found these treats, which had been packed to keep my energy up during labor, in a state of softened gooeyness. I immediately pointed out to Barb that these might better be stored in the fridge until It happened, but, alas, it was too late to save the Baby Ruth.

We've taken less stuff on a week's vacation. And I think the vacation was more fun.

The final two weeks were a lot less frantic than I had anticipated. I started my new job on July 14, and immediately told Margie, my secretary, and Sherry, the receptionist, to know where I was at all times in case my wife should call. Barbara called on July 17, just to say hello, but before she could say she was just calling to say hello, she sent everyone into a frenzy because, naturally, they didn't know where I was. This was not their fault; I had neglected to realize that they couldn't know where I was at all times unless I told them. From then on, whenever Barb called the office and got Margie or Sherry, the first thing she said was, "It's not time."

The week of July 14 was hot and muggy, and Barb was frustrated at having to stay in the air-conditioned apartment except for brief excursions to the deli or the bank. One night when I came home from work she vocalized these frustrations.

"Know what I did today?" she said.

"No, what?"

"I sat around like a lox."

The simile didn't make much sense when you thought about it, but the image seemed right somehow. .

The doctor made matters worse on Thursday of that week when he told Barb that he had detected a sudden jump in weight and blood pressure. This indicated a touch of toxemia and meant not only that Barbara would have to stay in the apartment but also that she'd have to stay in bed. I bought her a hand-held video game to keep her occupied. I felt sorry for her, even though I kept saying, "Remember all this when you want the next one."

"I'm so uncomfortable," she would moan.

"So give birth already," I'd tell her.

"Tell that to C.M."

So I'd lean over her considerable stomach and say, "Hey, C.M., this is your father speaking. Get out here."

I was summarily ignored.

Meanwhile, early gifts were pouring in. The creative department of my old agency threw me a going-away party and presented the cutest, tiniest Mets uniform, complete with cap. They also gave me a Bloomingdale's gift certificate with instructions to buy something for the baby or me. Being a responsible father-to-be, I bought something nice for the baby, although he or she really won't be able to wear the shirt until he or she is a teenager, so in the meantime I'll borrow it.

David and Mary Ann came up with three gifts: a little

running outfit; a set of bibs they had bought in Europe two years earlier because "we knew you'd get pregnant sooner or later"; and a plastic walker that allows the baby to sit down and move his or her legs and roll all over the place as though he or she were in one of the bumper cars at Coney Island. I knew this item would be a special favorite of our downstairs neighbors.

This last gift got me thinking about the cycles of human lives. Many baby implements are echoed with things old people use: The walker is one and, of course, a stroller is much like a wheel chair. Babies really make you get philosophical.

Meri brought a nursery monitor. This is a two-piece system: a transmitter for the nursery and a receiver for wherever the parents are. That way, even if the baby doesn't scream loud enough to wake the neighborhood, the parents can hear.

I understood the importance of this gift. I had already imagined myself lying awake nights wondering if the baby was crying, or gurgling, or breathing. It would make life easier, I thought, knowing I would know immediately if the baby's sleep had been disturbed. Not necessarily, Meri informed me. It seemed her husband, Joe, lay awake nights waiting for the receiver to make a sound. Oh well.

If Barbara got bored during her confinement period, she certainly had enough to read. We'd somehow gotten on parental mailing lists, and all the pregnancy books we'd accumulated were being replaced by a plethora of parenting publications and an invasion of mail-order offers for Sesame Street books and the like. (Who does that awful junk mail anyway? Whoops. . . .)

Among the available magazines to choose from were *Child, Parenting, Parents, Growing Child,* and *American Baby,* plus local ones like *Big Apple Parent* and *New York Family.* There was even *Grandparents* magazine for our parents.

It was obvious that the publishing business had discovered the new baby boom. It bothered me a bit to learn we were part of a big trend; I'd never thought of myself as being particularly trendy. I mean if I wanted to be trendy there were easier ways; I could simply wear Reebok sneakers and have margueritas at the latest Mexican restaurant. From a trend point of view, babies were a big risk anyway: What if you got pregnant, and then nine months later babies weren't in anymore?

Speaking of reading material, someone at my new job who doesn't have kids but somehow got on a parental mailing list gave me a catalog called *Constructive Playthings*. I immediately began shopping through it, looking for fun things I wanted to buy my kid. (By the way, I love shopping mail order. It's really the only way to go. You should buy everything mail order. Thank you in advance for your patronage.)

Anyway this catalog had some really interesting items in it, although what was "constructive" about them was not clearly evident. For instance, page 2, which is one of the really hot selling spaces in a catalog, was devoted to fake food, including:

REALISTIC PIZZA
8 slices of children's favorite food! This 12″ pizza has "pepperoni" and "sausage" pieces molded into the non-toxic, soft vinyl. Served on a real aluminum pizza pan.
$12.95

WHOLESOME DINNER SET
A nutritious, well-balanced meal: Steak, Peas, French Fries, Green Beans, and Milk in an unbreakable poly glass. Steak is 6″ long. All of life-size, authentically textured and colored, unbreakable, non-toxic, soft vinyl.
$36.95

Well it appeared somebody had solved that old fatty cell problem. If only my parents had been able to serve me vinyl food, I probably wouldn't have the weight problem I have today. I must question, however, the nutritional value of the "wholesome dinner set." And how come the word *delicious* never comes up in the descriptions?

On the next few pages of this catalog were various dolls, and it was obvious that anatomic correctness is a big feature in dolls these days. The Adam and Eva dolls, for example, not only had the words *anatomically correct sexual features* in the very first line of their descriptions but also were actually pictured with their little pants off, so that Adam's little thing was exposed for all the world to see.

I also found the Firebird "99" Dashboard, which was similar to the model I'd seen in Alan's and Carol's houses, except that it came with a CB radio. On the same page was a Super Disguise Kit, which I considered ordering in case there was a particularly troublesome period in my child's life during which I would want to slip in and out of the house incognito.

On a page called "Creating with Music," I discovered a five-piece rhythm set, which I believe is a sadistic thing even to manufacture much less sell to unsuspecting parents. As I had seen during my afternoon with little Elizabeth, toddlers can make quite enough noise banging on things that are not intended to be banged on without providing instruments intended solely for that purpose.

In case it sounds like this was an awful catalog, I should say that most of the items seemed delightful, and the appropriate ages for each item were conveniently included. On one pass through its pages, I figured I could easily spend about six zillion dollars. But not on fake pizza: I would go to Famous Ray's and buy a real one.

On July 24, Barbara's father drove into Manhattan in Gary's Blazer to deliver all the baby things we had purchased and stored in his house: crib, dressing table, and stroller. We spent the weekend assembling this stuff, a process which is not my strong point,* particularly when crib manufacturers include ten-step instructions and not all the parts. The absence of a small spring, for instance, stalled the completion of the

---

*When I finally discover what my strong point is, I'll be sure to let everyone know.

crib until Barb's dad could go back to the store on Long Island, pick up the spring, and deliver it to Manhattan.

A few days earlier, Fran and Rick had come down the hall to help us move furniture to make room for the baby; our wall system was now elled out from the wall to separate off the space by the window that was to be the baby's room. Into this space we crammed the crib, a dresser, the changing table, and the walker David and Mary Ann had brought. The place was really starting to look like a baby lived there. Or a juvenile furniture showroom.

On Saturday, July 26, we sat back and admired our work. We were ready for our baby. The baby, however, was apparently not ready for us.

July 27 came and went, marking the second straight weekend during which we had done absolutely nothing. I got cabin fever and went out for a walk and had some strange thoughts. I saw someone go by on a motorcycle and imagined myself zipping through the countryside on my Harley, a completely new and foreign fantasy, as the idea of going seventy miles an hour with nothing but a helmet between me and whatever might hit me was nothing to which I had ever aspired before. I attributed this strange thought to "weird things having a baby makes you do."

I realized that if I was going crazy spending two days at a time loitering in my apartment, Barbara, who had spent the last month perfecting the activity, must really be nuts. But knowing this did not prevent me from feeling sorry for myself as I sat in what was now our half of the living room, clicking through twenty-six cable TV channels and settling for roller derby.

Extra Innings

When I returned to the office on Monday, Margie informed me that her best friend, who was due on August 10, had delivered over the weekend. With only four hours of labor yet. That really pissed me off, and I immediately called Barbara to give her a piece of my mind. I was beginning to worry that Barbara and the baby were conspiring to give new meaning to the Labor Day holiday, but Barb assured me that they'd induce labor long before that.

"This baby's going to be a teenager by the time it comes out," I yelled. "If it's a boy, we'll be able to give it a bar mitzvah instead of a bris."

"It's not really late," Barbara said calmly. It amazed me how cool she was being about the whole thing. In fact the only thing that annoyed her was everybody calling to find out where the hell the baby was, as if they were becoming suspicious that the entire pregnancy had been an elaborate hoax to cover up Barbara's sudden propensity to gain huge amounts of weight or as if the baby was something that had been promised them and they had a right to complain about its tardy arrival.

I felt, however, that I *did* have the right to complain. "It certainly *is* late," I argued that evening when I got home. "It was due July 27. It's now July 28. It's late."

"But the original date was August 6."

Barbara was willing to give her doctor more slack than I was. I didn't think a medical degree was necessary to predict birth within a ten-day span. I mean here they are doing microsurgery as routinely as dispensing aspirin, and they can't pinpoint a birth date. Now the doctor was threatening a non–stress test at the hospital if nothing happened by the following week. It occurred to me that this was nothing but a clever ploy on his part, like when he threatened us with fertility drugs if we didn't conceive. It's quite brilliant really; it follows the same logic as lighting a cigarette while waiting for a bus because you just know that will make the bus come.

I tried to be understanding. After all, even in advertising, when we estimate a production job, we're allowed a 10-percent inaccuracy.

"Well, as long as it comes out before next weekend," I said. "I can't go through another weekend renting bad movies on videocassettes."

"Ooh, look," said Barbara, trying to change the subject. "Here's the baby's foot." She pointed at a protuberance on her stomach.

"Damn it, C.M.," I screamed. "You can't come out that way! Down! The exit is down! Jeez, our fetus is an idiot."

Barbara laughed. I found a wrestling talk show on cable.

Another weekend passed, and I thoroughly enjoyed my two big excursions: renting videotapes on Saturday and returning them on Sunday.

On Tuesday, August 5, we went to Beth Israel for the non–stress test. After prepaying downstairs, we went up to the fourth floor baby department and were ushered into delivery room one. A nurse told Barb to change into a delivery gown. Halfway through this process, the crack staff discovered that they had mixed up some forms and the woman who was about to give birth in the reception area was the one who should have been put in the delivery room, not Barbara. This made me wonder how far we could have gotten before they found out Barbara wasn't in labor and whether we could have had the baby right then and there by mistake.

Anyway we were taken to another room. A different nurse, Joyce, belted two gizmos to Barb's abdomen and two corresponding monitors perked up happily. One monitored the baby's heartbeat; the other picked up contractions which, surprisingly, were occurring fairly frequently. Barb had thought these were fetal movements, and I questioned her competence in identifying contractions.

"They don't hurt," she said.

"That's good," said the nurse.

The idea of the non–stress test is to compare the baby's heartbeat with the baby's movement as determined by Barb's pushing of a button. When the baby moves, the heartbeat gets faster. When it stops, the heartbeat goes back to its normal pace. The monitor prints out a graph that shows all this.

"Going by the Joyce rule," the nurse said, "it's a boy."

"What's the Joyce rule?" I asked.

"If the heartbeat sounds like a pony, it's a boy. If it sounds like a Whirlpool washing machine, it's a girl."

I listened carefully. I thought it sounded more like a washing machine, perhaps a Maytag. I told her this.

"That's the beauty of the Joyce rule. The rule is always right. But it's open to interpretation." Exacting medical science strikes again.

Our baby was pronounced healthy. (I thought it would be more appropriate to see if its parents would pass a stress test.) As Joyce wiped the connection glop off Barbara's stomach, she imparted another bit of highly scientific wisdom.

"If you want a surefire way to induce labor," she said, "eat lots of Chinese food with plenty of soy sauce."

This was the third old wives' tale we'd heard, and we filed it along with car rides on bumpy roads and having sex. On the way out of the room, I noticed a sonogram machine with a VCR attached to it.

"Some parents like to take home videotapes of the fetus," Joyce said, and I got angry that we hadn't even been able to get snapshots. I was especially upset because a videotape of the fetus would have been much more entertaining than most of the tapes I'd been renting on weekends.

That night we sat in the living room, and Barb had some fun with her newfound ability to distinguish minor contractions from the baby's movements. I was prepared to grasp at straws, so I began to time the contractions, but Barb refused to tell me when they were occurring.

"It's not time yet," she said. "They don't hurt."

"If it'll make you feel better I'll punch you in the stomach."

Barb had a glass of wine. The contractions stopped. August 6, the original due date, came and went, along with the page of my office calendar on which I had naively scribbled, eight and a half months earlier, "Baby due."

On Sunday, August 10, Meri, Joe, and four-month-old Lauren came into the city to keep us company. Meri thought that having a baby around would stir up Barbara's maternal instincts and bring on labor.

Incredibly she was right. Sort of.

As Lauren demonstrated her newfound ability to laugh (Meri and Joe were quite proud of this), Barbara calmly announced at 2:30 P.M. that she'd had a mild contraction. These contractions did not go away as they had in the past, but neither did they get stronger or more regular. By 4:30 P.M. Meri was ready to ignore this lack of strength and regularity and urged Barbara to call the doctor. I maintained that this wasn't what Stacy had told us to look for and that it was still too early to get the doctor involved. By 7:00 P.M., however, after Meri, Joe, and Lauren had packed themselves up and gone home, I decided I was tired of hearing Barbara time herself, and we called.

Minutes later the doctor called back. It sounded early, he said, but he sent us to the hospital to have an intern check it out.

Everything I had been worrying about regarding getting to the hospital and checking in went very smoothly. We remembered to take our overnight bag (with the candy bars from the refrigerator) and a pillow. We got a cab right away. The staff was waiting for us. We got one of the good delivery rooms. I even got my yellow gown on correctly. The only problem was that the baby didn't come out.

First a nurse asked us all sorts of questions and studiously entered the answers on a form. These questions sounded very much like the ones we'd answered on the preadmission papers that had been sent in months ago. It appeared the preadmission forms had been swallowed up in some abyss of hospital administration.

A different nurse, who seemed alarmingly preoccupied with watching "Punky Brewster" on the TV in the room (remember, this was the *good* room), hooked Barb up to the monitors. Then a doctor entered, put on the old glove, and dove in. "One centimeter," she announced. She went off to call Barb's doctor while the monitor beeped away.

A few minutes later, as I sat chomping on one of my candy bars, I was called to the phone to talk to Barb's doctor, who told me Barb was on her way, but it could be hours, even days yet. (Boy, these guys really loved making accurate predictions, didn't they?) He told us to go home and call him when the contractions were lasting about forty-five seconds (they had been going about twenty).

The intern returned to read the graph and unhooked the monitor. "You know," she said, "one of the nurses here has a theory that if the heartbeat sounds like a Whirlpool . . ." I interrupted and asked what it sounded like to her. "A pony," she said. Damn it, it still sounded like the wash cycle to me.

So we packed up and went home. We were now officially on red alert. It could be any minute. Or hour. Or day.

On Monday Gwen, who was visiting from Boston in the hopes of seeing a niece or nephew, stayed with Barb while I went to the office. I arrived around eight and frantically began arranging things so that the agency would be covered when I suddenly disappeared. This I had accomplished by ten. Then I called my mother to update her.

She avowed that she "just knew" something was going to happen the day before. She had spent the whole day at the pool club playing mah-jongg but facing the office in case we called. (She had seen to it that we had the phone number of the club.)

Before you attribute too much in the way of fortune-telling prowess to my mother, I should point out that this was only the latest in a series of similar premonitions to which both she and my father seemed prone. Two weeks earlier, they'd been out to a Chinese restaurant and had received a fortune cookie that said, "Good news will come to you tonight." Despite my parents' certainty that this could mean only one thing, the good news was most assuredly not forthcoming from Barb and me.

I ended the phone conversation with my nervous mom, who was off to do what she always did when she was nervous: the wash.

Having already cleared my desk for the entire week, I tried David at the office, but he was out. I even resorted to calling my grandparents, who pleasantly received the news of impending great-grandparenthood but couldn't keep the call going for much more than thirty seconds. With nothing else to do, and it being too early to go out to lunch, I did the only remaining thing that seemed reasonable.

I stared at the telephone.

It rang. Barb and Gwen had just returned from the doctor. He said It would probably happen later that day. I told Barb I would come home around two. Then I looked at my watch, realized that there was no way I'd be able to sit still for another two hours, and told Margie I was heading home now. She got all excited and started arranging an office pool. She figured she had an inside track since I'd told her the doctor said It would happen later that day.

Of course, she didn't know about the doctor's track record for predictions.

Chapter 7

THE BIRTH

OR

"Okay, Okay! You Don't Want to Breathe, You Don't Have to Breathe."

The Final Hours
(and Why I May Never Be an Uncle)

I arrived home from work to find Barbara and Gwen watching their own baby pictures, which Gwen had recently transferred to videotape. Gwen seemed extremely nervous. Barb seemed extremely uncomfortable. My first suggestion was to move the whole entourage from the living room to the bedroom, where Barbara could lie down.

The three of us began timing contractions. Barbara would call them out, then I'd look at my stopwatch and yell the time to Gwen, who'd write it down. The contractions hovered between forty and fifty-five seconds in duration and came three to six minutes apart. The doctor had said to call when the contractions lasted forty-five seconds, but Barb still didn't seem to be in enough pain. Her back hurt quite a bit, though, so I got my racquetball out of the overnight bag and rolled it on her spine.

By 3:00 P.M. the contractions were more or less regular, and Barb seemed to be putting more effort into her moaning, so I called the doctor and told the nurse about the contractions.

"So when are you going to the hospital?" she asked.

"Aren't you supposed to tell me?" Between this, and the washing machines, and the soy sauce, I was really losing faith in the medical profession. I figured next baby I'd try a lawyer. Maybe we could have the whole pregnancy and birth negotiated.

The doctor told us to come to the office. This we did, instructing Gwen to stay home with the overnight bag.

After a two-block cab ride, the doctor put on the glove and announced, "Two centimeters. Still plenty to go. Probably near midnight."

We walked home. Our doorman, who had seen us leave and return the night before, was immensely disappointed to see us again.

So was Gwen, who was so disillusioned by the experience that she was rethinking her plans to have Roy father a child in the near future. When Karen called to check in Gwen passed on this new thinking, and the chances of my becoming an uncle became suddenly slim.

At 4:30 P.M. Barb's dad stopped by to pick Gwen up. As they left, Gwen seemed to sigh in relief as if to say, "Thank God It didn't happen while I was here."

I didn't have that luxury. I didn't need that luxury. Because I had no sooner notified everyone to be on standby alert, than the contractions became weaker, shorter, and less regular.

Barb took a shower to let hot water spill onto her breasts (which was supposed to get labor going). I watched the Mets game. By eleven, the game was over but it seemed as though whoever had thrown out the first ball of labor had taken it back.

C.M. had changed his or her mind.

At 11:15 P.M. Barb found a few drops of moisture in bed and we debated whether or not her water had broken. The doctor called in midargument, so I asked him.

"Is it a continuous trickle?" he asked me.

"Is it continuous?" I asked Barb.

"No," she told me.

"No," I told the doctor.

"Did she sneeze or cough just before?" the doctor asked me.

"Did you sneeze or cough?" I asked Barb, and then, in a whisper, "or fart?"

Barb shook her head no, and I heard the doctor lauging. "Oh, you heard that, huh?"

"Yes," he said. "Keep up your sense of humor. Call me if they get regular."

Right after he hung up, Barb had her bloody show. I couldn't quite recall what this meant, but I had the feeling it was signifigant. "Quick, call the doctor back," I said.

"No need," said Barb, who had one of her books out. "That just indicates that things might start happening faster now. That in itself is not a reason to call the doctor."

Considering that *nothing* had happened for the past seven hours, something happening faster seemed very promising. At that point I would have welcomed any event that moved faster, even if it was my hair falling out.

I sat around waiting for something to happen. Barb went to sleep. I hadn't slept for three days. (The night before, Barb had accidentally rolled over onto me and nearly broken my back. Then she spent the rest of the evening snoring in a way that seemed imitative of wild jungle noises.)

I went into the living room and watched Australian football on cable.

At 2:00 A.M. Barbara was in agony and the contractions seemed pretty regular. We called the doctor. The doctor called back. He sent us to the hospital.

The candy bars went back in the bag. The bag, the pillow, and Barb and I found a cab. Off we went.

There was bad news waiting at the hospital. Only the dreaded room eight was available. We couldn't even have that until we answered some questions from the admitting nurse, questions that sounded awfully like the ones we had answered on our last visit, which had sounded extremely similar to the ones on the preadmission forms.

"We filled out those forms last night," I announced.

The nurse looked through the file. "Last night?" she asked suspiciously, as if I might be trying to put one over on her.

"Yes," I said. "We were just here Sunday night."

"Oh, Sunday night. *Two* days ago." I'd forgotten we were past midnight and that it was now Tuesday. "We have to fill them out again." This puzzled me as the information, stuff like Barbara's birth date, was not particularly time sensitive. There was nothing that would have changed from Sunday to Tuesday.

A few minutes later the monitors were plugged in again and another intern's fingers were in action. Barbara didn't like this doctor because he had big fingers and because, as she later told me, "He just stuffed them in there. He didn't even introduce himself."

I watched the monitor graph Barb's pain for about three hours while I munched a candy bar and helped her breathe through the contractions. It's a little strange watching someone's pain being printed on a little piece of paper. Then she was unhooked. Nope, not yet. In fact Barb had regressed back to one centimeter, although she claimed that was because of this doctor's thicker fingers. The intern began berating Barb's pain threshold, stopping just short of accusing my wife of crying wolf.

This bothered me. Even with Stacy's classes and all, there was no way for Barb to know which pains were the really bad ones. Every contraction seemed worse than the last. How could she know how much agony she was supposed to be in when she had no basis for comparison? Something else bothered me, too. I worried that by the time It happened for real I'd be out of candy bars.

We got home around six. I put Barb in bed and went down to the all-night coffee shop to get some breakfast to go. I returned to find her watching MTV. We ate breakfast. We breathed through some more contractions, which I timed and entered in my log.

At 8:45, we set off for our regular 9:00 A.M., Tuesday doctor's appointment (after giving Fran the keys to our apartment so that she'd be able to bring the overnight bag to the hospital in case the doctor sent us right over there as we hoped).

Barb's doctor added his finger to the parade of digits that had entered my wife over the past few days and immediately sent us home with instructions to fix ourselves stiff drinks and go to sleep. He wanted the contractions to go away so we could start all over again, not an entirely attractive prospect as Barb had already been having contractions for about forty-three hours. The idea of sleep wasn't a bad one, however, since it was an experience that had eluded us for about three days.

It was a double Kahlua for Barb, a shot of Sambucca for me. We dozed for an hour and a half before the contractions woke her up. We called the doctor, who now recognized my voice.

"Come to the office," he said. "I'll drive you to the hospital."

Here we go again. Candy bars in overnight bag. Pillow under arm. Get a cab. Drive two blocks.

The doctor bustled us into his new Volvo, which was, surprisingly (and illegally), parked right in front of the office. He didn't really like his new Volvo, he told us as we drove. He thought it was underpowered. Barb and I didn't really care.

Thank God they didn't ask us to fill in the forms again. We got room five, not terrible, not great. In spite of my objections (as per Stacy's instructions), I was implored to remain by admitting while Barbara got undressed and hooked up. I sat there with the overnight bag and pillow while a sixteen-year-old Hispanic girl's water broke and poured onto the floor. It smelled like fish. Nobody on the staff appeared to notice. I looked down the corridor of doors, numbered one through eight, and listened to occasional screams coming anonymously from them. I felt like the stereotypical patient in a dentist's waiting room. I told that to Barb's doctor as he passed by me. He told me he hadn't been to the dentist for twelve years.

Here was the game plan, as explained by the doctor.

They were going to give her an anaesthetic called an epidural, which was essentially a spinal block and would remove most of the pain. It would also remove the need for a breathing coach, so I'd have nothing to do but sit and watch and eat my candy bars. The doctor hoped she would dilate on her own at least enough so he could rupture the water bag. If she didn't, they would then give her something called Pitocin, which would induce the last stage of labor.

Thus informed I went into room five to find the monitors hooked up and beeping away. A few minutes later, an Asian anaesthesiologist told Barbara to lie on her side facing me. He went around behind her and worked feverishly for quite awhile. He looked like he was knitting a sweater. When he was finished, there was a cross-shaped pattern of surgical tape on Barbara's back with a tube running beneath it like an electrical extension cord somebody had covered with an area rug. Soon, Barbara felt much better.

"Now we just wait," said the doctor. "This is not a normal labor."

That was not a profound revelation, considering we were now entering the third day.

And so we waited. I ate another candy bar. I was glad that I had never actually stopped smoking, because I would have started again anyway. The *surgeon general* would smoke under these conditions. I went to a deli across the street and got a sandwich. I bought a crossword puzzle magazine and sat in the room doing word searches, which were the hardest puzzles I was capable of handling at that point.

Around six, Barb was up to five centimeters, but was not really progressing. In went the Pitocin. Then we waited some more.

I began looking for connect-the-dots pictures in my magazine.

It Happens

At eight Barb was at eight centimeters. The doctor explained that the water bag was in a bad position and was preventing the baby from falling into place. So, with the rounded crochet hook Stacy had shown us, he broke the water. A brownish liquid came gushing out between Barb's legs.

"It shouldn't be brown," he said. "That means the baby was in distress and defecated in the uterus. If I had to guess now, I'd say we'll end up with a C-section, but we want to give it every opportunity to come out by itself." With that, he left the room, leaving me to change the blue pads under Barbara whenever puddles of the brown stuff began to form.

I didn't remember Stacy saying anything about the coach changing blue pads with brown, fishy liquid on them.

I'd rather breathe.

However, I'd rather change blue pads with brown, fishy liquid on them than go through what was about to happen next, which was the scariest hour I've ever experienced.

I'd been watching the heartbeat monitor, and I'd noticed it was declining steadily but not particularly rapidly. I was reluctant to call anybody's attention to this as I had spent a good part of the evening calling their attention to other things I'd thought were wrong, like a red light flashing on the intravenous machine. Besides I knew they were monitoring everything out at the desk. Around eight thirty, Barb's doctor's partner came in, glanced at the monitor, and said, "This is ridiculous. We have to go in." Then Barb's doctor came in, and his partner repeated this alarming statement for his benefit. These two doctors are an odd couple; Barb's is a laid-back, sort of California type. His partner is more the high-strung, New York Jewish, neurotic type. And so, while the partner was saying terrifying things like "fetal distress," Barb's doctor was telling me to bring my camera and follow him to the operating room.

Suddenly people were running all over, and racing with her bed down the hall. Slinging my camera around my neck, I followed the careening bed, passing a whole bunch of anxious fathers who had stepped out into the corridor to see what the commotion was about. They all had cameras around their necks, too. We must have looked like a nervous Japanese tour group.

The operating room was an eerie place that felt cold and lifeless like a meat locker. Even the lighting was cold. I would have been even more terrified if Stacy hadn't shown us the room on our tour.

I was given my mask, cap, and shoecovers and told to sit by Barbara's head. As I stoked her hair, the sheets were crafted into an effective screen so that neither I nor Barb could see what was happening below her chin, which, I can assure you, was nothing that I intended to go out of my way to do. (When I did take a peek accidentally, I saw an unidentifiable organ sticking out of Barb's belly. She now says I know her intimately inside and out.)

I can't tell you much about the operation, as I was focused entirely on soothing Barbara, figuring she had to be some exponent of scared more than I was, and I was scared to the fifth or sixth power. If you've ever seen a medical TV show, that's about the size of it.

Barb and I shivered in the cold, heavy, dead air. The doctors told Jewish American Princess jokes, all of which I'd heard before.

"How does a JAP eat a banana?" Barb's doctor asked. "Sorry, I need my hands for the punchline, and they're busy." His partner was saying, "Cut here, grab that," and the like.

And then . . . crying.

"Congratulations," the doctor said. "It's a healthy girl."

Incredibly my first thought was, "I *knew* it was a washing machine."

I watched the nurses carry a large pink thing over to a table in the corner while I heard myself saying, "Her name is Casey."

"Eight pounds, ten ounces!" somebody yelled.

This sure as hell was not a small baby!

"Well, go take pictures." The doctor's voice was muffled because his head was involved in sewing (actually stapling) my wife together. I told Barb to stay calm and went over to the baby. "Don't forget the lens cap," the doctor called.

I unscrewed the lens cap and looked down at this pink, rubbery thing with a clothespin in its navel. She was crying like an angry cat. Her foot was purple from the footprint the nurse had just taken. Her other foot and hands were blue. She had a full head of red hair matted to her scalp. Her pudgy cheeks were orange from screaming.

She was gorgeous. I took my pictures and returned to Barbara.

Minutes later a nurse handed me a swaddled, screeching bundle. I took it gingerly in my arms and said, as if I were still talking to Barbara's stomach, "Hi, Casey, this is Daddy."

And incredibly, amazingly, beautifully, she stopped crying.

Her eyelids opened wide, and she stared at me with cloudy, blue-green eyes. My finger glided over her cheek; it was the softest thing I'd ever touched. The feel of her hair, which I could now see had light blonde streaks in it (the nurse said it was Barb's color hair not knowing that Barb's hair is dyed), was indescribable; there is no material on earth to compare to it.

And I am crying as I write this.

I reluctantly handed her back to the nurse and followed Barb into the recovery room, which seemed to be rather makeshift in nature. There were a lot of makeshift things in labor that night; they were filled beyond capacity. I stood by helplessly as Barbara shivered violently and groaned in pain. I tried to get her to breathe with me, but she refused with a frightened "Not now," and I meekly backed down from my request. A shot of morphine calmed her down, but immediately gave me something new to worry about: I had visions of my wife as an addict on a street corner in the Bowery.

Then we heard screeching, and our daughter (*our* daughter) was wheeled in in a clear bassinet. She screamed as the nurse lifted her and put her in Barbara's arms.

"Hello, Casey," Barbara cooed. "It's Mommy."

Silence. Our baby girl virtually melted into her mother's trembling arms. Then the nurse took her away to be measured in the nursery.

An hour passed. I sat holding Barb's hand and eating one of my few remaining candy bars. A nurse brought me coffee. What was going to happen next?

Barb asked the nurse what to do if she wanted to throw up. The nurse produced a yellow, plastic curved bowl and instructed her to turn her face to the side and heave into it. Then she went to attend another patient, and I was left holding the bowl. This was difficult as I could barely stand myself; I ended up collapsed on the chair ready to jump at Barb's slightest cough, as though it were my life's work to have that bowl in place.

At that moment, it *was* my life's work.

Folks, my wife is the bravest woman on earth. Any woman who goes through that is brave. Women are nuts to want a baby in the first place, courageous to go through with it, and insane enough to forget the whole thing as soon as that miracle is placed in their arms.

When Barb got drowsy, I went into the lobby to make two eagerly awaited phone calls. My parents were relieved and elated. Barb's father exhibited uninhibited joy that was totally uncharacteristic to the family. As he repeated the news, I heard Gwen, Karen, and Gary cheering in the background.

By midnight the morphine was wearing off. But another shot was not forthcoming, as Barb would soon be moved to a room, and for some reason that is beyond understanding she could not be moved if she was asleep.

After I spent ten frantic minutes harassing the one poor nurse on duty in that busy, noisy room, a big woman with a mustache materialized to roll Barb up to a semiprivate room that was the very last room available that night.

I waited until a second morphine injection put Barb to sleep, wearily found my way to the street, hailed a cab, and went home to sleep for the first time in three days. Before I hit the sack I slipped a note under Fran and Rick's door, and I changed the outgoing message on our answering machine to: "Casey Ingrid Hallen was born at 9:19 P.M., August 12, 1986, weighing in at a huge eight pounds, ten ounces."

And then I went happily to sleep.

Chapter 8

Our First Days as a Family

OR

"Forget Every Baby You've Ever Seen— <u>Ours</u> Is the Most Beautiful, Cutest, Best Baby That's Ever Been Swaddled. Don't Even Think That You Have Even the Remotest Chance of Having a Baby That Can Even Come Close."

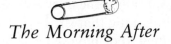

The Morning After

I'd told Barb that I just had to sleep as late as I wanted the next day, but before I got into bed, I set my alarm for 8:00 A.M. Barbara knew I would and called me at 8:15 to inform me that the first feeding was at 9:00. I raced to the hospital.

Barbara looked bad but better than the night before. Of course there are probably lepers who look better than Barbara had the night before. She was pleased, however, by her reduced girth. Instead of looking pregnant, she now looked like she drank a lot of beer.

A nurse rolled in a cart and there was Casey, about the same as I'd remembered her except with a T-shirt on under the blanket. The nurse read off the number on the tiny bracelet around Casey's wrist to confirm that it matched Barbara's number. I remarked that the matching bracelets would make nice mementos. (I found I was suddenly into mementos. I had

131

already decided to save my two remaining candy bars for posterity.)

The nurse put Casey under Barb's arm, and Barb's breasts fulfilled the dream they'd been training for. After five minutes on each nipple, I got to burp her (Casey, not Barbara) by sitting her on my knee and leaning her forward with her jaw cupped in my hand. Casey obliged eagerly and then looked at me with a rather befuddled expression, as though the burp had surprised her.

This was the first time I had held my daughter without being in a state of panic, and I took in every feature: the fat cheeks, the double chin, the tiny fingers and fingernails, the blonde highlights in her hair, and the button nose. (The last was, we were sure, sister Karen's. Casey was definitely a Tamarkin.) She stared back with equal interest until the nurse came to retrieve her.

Meanwhile Barb's roommate, who had also had a C-section the night before (almost as if the hospital were having a special on them), was complaining that she hadn't received her child, which the staff seemed to be having trouble locating. She was also telling the nurse that she hadn't been given her painkiller.

"Didn't you give her the Demerol?" the nurse asked another nurse.

"I thought that was for next door," the second nurse said.

I decided I had to get Barb a private room at all costs.

It was at all costs: $185 extra a day, to be exact, for the private deluxe room, which was the only private room available.

It was worth every penny.

If your hospital has such a room and you can afford it, I highly recommend it. Particularly after the harrowing evening we'd had, this room provided a soothing atmosphere for recovering, having visitors, and getting to know our baby. There was a 19-inch color TV (instead of the miniature jobs on the swiveling arms), and a sofabed, and a refrigerator that they stocked with soda and juice. There were prints on the wall and an Oriental rug. There were two phones. There was a view of a park. The place could have gone for about $150,000 as a co-op.

I called Sharon, my secretary at the old agency, and she immediately sent out a memo. I called Margie, my secretary at the new agency, and she immediately went to see who'd won the office pool. Flowers arrived and balloons.

Still Barbara was exhausted. She barely got past the one o'clock feeding, which I supplemented with a bottle of glucose water.

Later a Doctor Goldsomething introduced himself as the pediatrician and told us he had examined Casey and she was just fine except for a fatty lump in her ear, which would probably fade away. That made us feel great, except that we had no idea who this guy was. When *our* pediatrician showed up, he was embarrassed to see some other doctor's name on Casey's crib card (the one that says "I'm a Girl!"—ultimately, I got to keep this card as a memento), and shyly asked us if we really wanted him. A quick check of hospital records showed his name on all the forms, including the ones we'd filled out two nights in a row. Who was this fraud Goldsomething? What did he want with our daughter? It turned out the hospital had assigned him by mistake. Well at least they hadn't assigned a proctologist.

Soon it was three o'clock. Visiting hour. I met my mom, Barb's dad, and Gwen for lunch and then took them to the room. Karen met us there. Barb and I described every move Casey had made—every sigh, every sound, every burp.

At 3:45 I led everyone down the hall for showtime in the nursery. All the babies were turned toward the window so that we could see how much more beautiful Casey was than the rest of those scrawny, misshapen kids. Casey was real easy to pick out; she was the only redhead there. She was also twice the size of the others. The five of us put our noses to the glass and watched Casey sleep.

We all had tears in our eyes.

That night Grandpa Stan and Aunt Gwen were back, along with my father, Grandpa Bernie, and my grandparents. All the stories were repeated. Everyone sighed at the nursery window as Stan snapped pictures through the glass. And then I saw something I'll never forget: the two grandfathers staring into the room, waving at their little granddaughter and congratulating themselves. It brought tears to my eyes. (I'd suddenly developed an alarming tendency to have tears in my eyes. It usually happened whenever I held my daughter. I hoped this tendency would go away before she started bringing dates home to meet her parents.)

The nine o'clock feeding was difficult: Barb was tired, and Casey was fussy. We'd told everyone how good she was and how she responded to our voices, but that night she seemed intent on trying out every cry she had, including one piercing shriek that would scare a gorilla. Mercifully the nurse appeared to take her away, and I was struck by how good an idea that was. Wouldn't it be great if, after you went home with the baby, you could ring a bell whenever the kid got annoying, and someone would come and take her away? Hmm, there's a business in that, I think.

Around ten thirty, I went home to sleep. Barbara was snoring before I was out the door. I lay in bed thinking about what Casey would look like when she was, say, eleven. How old would she have to be before I allowed her to date? I figured twenty, twenty-five would be a good age.

The Days After the Morning After

On Thursday Casey spent most of the day in the room with us, which allowed us to do lots of fun things for the first time, like change her diapers. I tried once, and although I was okay with the diaper, I was an absolute clod with the swaddling. Barbara, on the other hand, took to it like, well, like a mother. She was going to be a great mother.

Meanwhile, I took lots of pictures. Then I ran out to a one-hour photo developer and ordered lots of prints.

Back at the hospital, Barbara told me she'd seen Casey smile.

"Remember what Stacy said," I commented. "They don't really react to stimuli that way. What looks like a smile is really gas."

"No," said Barbara. "The nurses say she does it all the time. They say they're really smiles."

As if to prove Barbara's point, Casey widened her eyes and opened her mouth in what had to be the world's sunniest expression. I almost got the feeling she was laughing at me.

She really did seem to be a good baby. She never cried just because she was cranky; she was either hungry, gassy, or wet. The only really annoying habit she had was falling asleep at the nipple; Barb had all she could do to keep her awake long enough to feed her.

I regretted all my old baby jokes. Casey was going to be Daddy's little girl. I wondered when I'd be able to get to FAO Schwarz to buy the largest stuffed animal in the store.

In the afternoon a new doctor came in. He was a plastic surgeon the pediatrician had called in to look at Casey's ear. He said the small lump was cartilage that had folded over in the womb. It might go away, or he could cut it out quickly when she was around five years old. I told him to send us a postcard in five years.

That night I tried to get Casey to watch the Mets game with me. She didn't seem interested. Well it *was* a boring game.

Friday morning, Casey was wide awake, and as I held her her rubbery face went through its whole repertoire of expressions while Barb snapped Polaroids. Casey often hiccoughed after feeding (because she sucked too quickly, the doctor said), but she never seemed bothered by it. She did look funny, though, because her whole body bounced when she did it. She also sneezed, a process that involved the caving in of her little face followed by the cutest little "CHEW!"

Have I mentioned how adorable our baby was?

Later in the morning, I bought a box of chocolate IT'S A GIRL cigars (I later saved the empty box as a memento) and, armed with a dozen or so photographs, headed uptown, first to my old agency, then to my new one.

The people at my new agency commented that she was definitely the cutest baby they'd ever seen, but I modestly chalked these rave reviews up to their desire to suck up to one of the big honchos. The people at my old agency, however, who had nothing to gain politically by being nice to me, made similar comments, thus giving credence to my personal belief that Casey was the world's most precious baby.

That afternoon my parents and Barb's dad were up, and we found out that the nurses would allow grandparents in the room with the baby, providing they were thoroughly scrubbed and gowned. (Both grandpas, however, declined our invitation to be in the room during feeding.) Everyone got to hold Casey. My father seemed the most anxious about this; he was really afraid he might drop her. (He is, in fact, not very handy.) Finally he sat on the couch and held his arms out stiffly as we put the warm bundle into his hands. There's a Yiddish word, *kvelled,* which, like many Yiddish words, has no direct translation. Nevertheless kvelled is what all the grandparents— actually, all the relatives—did.

The critics raved:

> "She's perfect, and I'm not just saying that because she's my granddaughter."
>
> *Grandpa Bernie*

> "I can't wait to be her favorite aunt."
>
> *Aunt Karen*

> "The people at the pool club brought back other people to see the pictures."
>
> *Grandma Sunny*

> "Well worth the wait."
>
> *Grandpa Stan*

After visiting hours we went to the apartment to unpack the layette that my parents had picked up on the way to the hospital. There were all kinds of tiny outfits, plus sheets and quilts and a digital thermometer and a comb-and-brush set. Dad and Karen spent an hour or so trying to figure out how the bumper guards attached to the crib. Meanwhile I straightened up the remnants of our final pre-Casey days at home. I threw away the scattered sheets of legal paper with contraction timings on them. I found my racquetball under the bed. I discarded half a slice of toast from that Tuesday morning bring-in breakfast.

Then we filled the drawers with all the stuff from the layette. We now had everything in our nursery except a baby and a mommy.

Saturday was a boring day, except for a visit from the pediatrician with the news that our baby had taken one of the biggest shits the people in the nursery had ever seen. Barbara and I beamed with pride.

The only visitors that day were David and Mary Ann, who brought a photo album that was already too small for our rapidly swelling pile of snapshots. They both listened as I told all my tales of Casey's accomplishments and marveled at my lightning-fast adaptation to fatherhood.

"Hey, mate," said David, "you still going to cook the baby when we come over for dinner?"

I glowered at him for even suggesting such a thing.

The Family Comes Home

Sunday was to be homecoming day for Barb and Casey. It began early in the morning when Barbara's staples were removed. (I yelled at her for not saving them as mementos.) I arrived at the hospital around nine and we waited for Barb's doctor to come and release her, which he did about ten thirty.

Then, while Barb showered and dressed, I went to check out, a chore I'd been dreading, considering the hospital's previous foul-ups regarding records. It was, however, a surprisingly painless process; all I had to do was pay the $10 phone bill and get a couple of pink slips from the cashier. One of these I turned in at the nurses' desk, the other at the nursery, along with a bag of clothes intended for Casey's trip home.

Stan and Karen arrived at eleven thirty and Karen snapped pictures as the nurses dressed Casey in her pink jumpsuit and receiving blanket. A white, frilly bonnet completed the outfit, and all the nurses said goodbye to what Barb and I assumed to be their favorite baby.

Casey was great in the car, fascinated with new things to look at.

She was a tad fussy at home. Barb tried to feed her in the bedroom while I unpacked the overnight bag and the care packages the hospital had given us (diapers, little bottles of sterile water, breast pads, sanitary napkins, pacifiers, and so on). Then we put her in her new crib to sleep.

She looked so tiny in the crib, compared to the much smaller bassinet she'd slept in at the hospital. Through the afternoon, her body revolved clockwise until she was lying horizontally across the mattress.

Bernice, the live-in nurse that Aunt Ellen and Uncle Joe were paying for, arrived at one o'clock. She was a large woman with a West Indian accent like Stacy's and immediately revealed herself to be an ardent Mets fan, which endeared her to me.

We spent an hour watching the game with the Cardinals, and for that hour life was no different from, say, two weeks earlier, except that there was now a baby by the window and a big black woman in a white uniform sitting on our couch.

Then Bernice sent Karen, Dad, and me out on errands. There were baby things to be bought: formula, alcohol, lotions, a bathtub, a garbage can for diapers, and lunch for us.

Casey was terrific. She slept most of the afternoon. Then Barb fed her, we played with her awhile, and Bernice put her back in the crib. Bernice made herself comfortable with the cable TV in the living room while Barb and I went to bed, watched *The China Syndrome* for awhile, and fell asleep, myself somewhat more fitfully than Barb, as she had herself propped up on about twenty pillows in an attempt to alleviate some of the discomfort from the operation.

We were all ready to start life with baby — and, for the first week, Bernice.

Our daughter is a genius! I came home from work on Monday to find her dressed in a multicolored striped jumper and to hear glowing reports from Barb and Bernice about her accomplishments. She had, for instance, managed to propel herself from one end of the crib to the other with a caterpillarlike, pre-crawl motion, made possible only by her ability to hold her head up for long periods of time. She had also been observed to respond to speech with imitative cooing noises of her own.

All of the above actions, said Bernice, were more appropriate for a baby six *weeks* old than for one six *days* old.

I was so proud.

I also felt a bit guilty as Barb and Bernice dressed our daughter in her yellow nightgown. (The sleeves were about three inches longer than her arms and she seemed to delight in flopping the loose ends around.) Were we providing enough stimuli for our future Mensa member? Someone had given us a crib mobile as a gift, and I quickly attached it so that Casey could stare at the brightly colored butterflies.

"Doesn't it play music?" Bernice asked.

"Uh, no," I replied.

"Doesn't it turn around?" Bernice inquired.

"I believe not."

"It just sits there?" Bernice questioned.

I was getting the idea that this mobile fell somewhat short of expectations. "No good, huh?" Bernice just sort of clicked her tongue in response.

I knew that a mobile wasn't all that appropriate yet anyway, since Casey didn't lie on her back yet, so she couldn't look at it. We needed something she could look at while she was on her side, something to keep her fascinated, something she could learn from. We needed a crib mirror. We needed interesting patterns. We needed soothing noises.

We needed them now!

I came home one night to find an especially cranky daughter and a nurse and wife who seemed intent on testing Daddy's ability to cope with prolonged periods of shrill crying.

Barb and Bernice handed me Casey and sat on the couch staring at me, as if my attempts at quieting my daughter would be immensely entertaining. I tried all methods of pacification, including shaking a rattle, bouncing her on my knee, giving her a bottle of water (Casey absolutely hated water—she would literally shove the bottle away with her little hand), and even, as a last resort, singing. None of these resulted in more than ten seconds of silence.

I looked over at the couch to find an unabashedly amused audience.

I then took a new approach. I imitated Casey's cry. If she wailed, I wailed. If she shrieked, I shrieked. If she made her hesitant hiccoughy sounds, so did I. This did not make Casey stop crying, but the doubling of the noise factor annoyed Barb and Bernice enough that they took the baby away from me.

"Well," I said to Barb, "if this is the worst it gets, I'll be all right." I had weathered the onslaught quite well, I thought.

"I don't think it's the worst," Barb said.

Bernice shook her head.

Bernice had this irritating habit of looking smug anytime anyone did anything around Casey. It was as though she were saying, "Sure, you may think she's cute while I'm bearing the brunt of the work, but just wait. . . ."

And, of course, it *was* Bernice who would stay up all night when Casey did. And it *was* Bernice who was changing the diapers. And it *was* Bernice who would pacify Casey until feeding time, because we were determined that the baby would eat when *we* wanted her to so that we could get her onto a manageable schedule.

And while Bernice was doing all that, Barb and I took pictures.

Casey was at her best immediately after her 8:00 P.M. feeding. That's when I would play with her and watch her smile and try to figure out exactly what she was staring at over my shoulder. I told Bernice these brief encounters every evening made all the work worthwhile. Bernice just said, "Work? Just wait till next week."

An Open Letter to the President of Toys Я Us

Dear Sir or Madam:

This is a plea from a beleaguered father. Please, please, please open a store in Manhattan.

I know the rent is high here, but, believe me, you can more than make it up by charging premium prices to parents who are starving for toys. And there are so many of us. I just spent a week on an overcrowded nursery floor, so I know. And when you take into account all the pregnant women I see walking around, you'll be getting new customers every day.

You could probably come out even on my business alone.

Just the other day, I became obsessed with the idea of obtaining stimulation for my newborn daughter, Casey. I went everywhere looking for a simple crib mirror. No luck. And forget about a turning musical mobile. It took me three days to find one of those, and it still wasn't exactly the one I wanted.

Meanwhile Fran and Rick, our friends down the hall who also have a house in New Jersey and therefore have access to one of your stores, came home with the entire Babycise gymnasium, including barbells and exercise mats and even a videotape. I admit I thought it was a tad silly, especially the part about giving your baby a massage, but the point is, they could get all this great stuff and we're stuck with whatever the schlock stores on Fourteenth Street are selling.

It's unfair! I demand that you stop discriminating against Manhattanites. I look forward to seeing one of your stores in the near future, preferably replacing at least six of the fruit stands in our neighborhood. (After all, how much fruit can we eat?)

Thank you for your kind attention.

Defenseless

On Friday Casey's shriveled umbilical cord fell off, leaving behind an adorable inny. The shedding of the cord (Barb threw it away despite my pleas to save it as a memento) was not only a big milestone in Casey's life, it also meant, we knew, that Bernice's stay with us was coming to its end.

With the cord off, Bernice could now show us how to bathe the baby, the last of her responsibilities. We knew she had another job the next week, and would want to get a few nights' sleep between jobs.

What was most amazing to me was that Barbara and I felt more-or-less prepared to go it alone.

Barbara had found a great trick that made Casey go to sleep: She'd turn on the radio and dance around with her. It even worked for me, despite my aforementioned lack of rhythm and my total inability to do even a box step without stumbling. Casey ignored my gracelessness, which made sense, since she wasn't exactly great at dipping herself. Bernice was thoroughly amused at this song-and-dance spectacle and laughed heartily for hours afterward.

On Saturday night, we put the yellow plastic baby bath across the kitchen sink and filled it with lukewarm water.

"Now you'll hear some crying," Bernice warned.

But it wasn't that bad. Casey seemed to feel that it was

appropriate to cry but couldn't really think of a good reason to do so, and so we heard only half-hearted hysterics as Bernice dipped her in the water and ran the washcloth over her pink body.

On Sunday morning, after hugs and kisses and promises to stay in touch, Bernice was on her way.

And we were on our own!

As I have said, Barb and I were not all that apprehensive about being left alone with Casey. But what did we know?

I'd arranged to take our first Berniceless week off from work to help Barbara and get to know my daughter. This was not exactly the most relaxing vacation I've ever had. By Wednesday, I had attained that sort of walking sleep state you usually find yourself in the day after an all-night New Year's Eve party.

Judging from the baby horror stories I'd heard, Casey seemed pretty good. She slept through a good deal of the night, but Barb and I both *imagined* we heard her crying even when she wasn't. When we weren't dancing around with her waiting for her to go to sleep, we were checking her crib to see why she wasn't making any noise. I was beginning to see why almost all parents are neurotic.

Casey's crying, even the now-perfected banshee wail, never lasted much more than a half hour. The day after Bernice left, Casey and her parents had their first challenge match, wherein she demanded to be fed an hour earlier than we were prepared to oblige. Barb and I were determined to win this first confrontation. We did not ignore the baby and her irrational crying; we bounced her in our arms and attempted to reason with her using sound, calm arguments that conveyed our point of view. After thirty minutes, Casey had cried herself into an exhausted sleep.

Ah, the thrill of victory.

This contest gave us the confidence to meet the coming days and months head on (that, and the somewhat disturbing discovery that our brilliant daughter could be quieted for an hour at a time by placing her in front of a television playing music videos).

We spent our days simply watching Casey as she struggled to move about in her crib, as she focused on various objects, as she drooled all over the place. It sometimes surprised us to realize that although she resembled a miniature human being, functionally she was more like a puppy.

There were hours of sheer joy, when Casey was performing none of her main activities (eating, sleeping, and crying) and we could have nearly rational play periods. She seemed to try to imitate our repeated actions like kissing or sticking our tongues out. She made little sounds that appeared to indicate she was onto our game. Were we imagining all this, just as we were imagining phantom cries in the night? Who knows. But it made us very happy nonetheless. These little games were indications that the rewards our future held for us would greatly outweigh the aggravation.

We both imagined Casey saying her first words, taking her first steps, going off to school, borrowing the car, and using contraceptives. Considering that Casey hadn't yet progressed beyond moving clockwise in her crib, we had pretty good imaginations.

Those of you out there who are already parents are probably thinking, "Just wait till they see what happens next." Those of you who are pregnant are probably thinking, "What the hell is going to happen next." Those of you who are not pregnant are probably thinking, "Boy, am I glad we're not pregnant."

Of course Barb and I don't know what will happen next. We *do* know that I take after my father in the photographic department. (We have a photo of what I think is the ceiling of Barb's hospital room.) And we have made the decision actually to drive to Westchester and maybe even contact a real estate broker.

But beyond that, we don't know a damned thing. And the only way you'll know what happens to us next is if the publisher asks me to write a sequel, which he will only do if a lot of people buy this book, in which case my daughter can have her own phone.

So please. If you liked this book, do *not* pass it on to your friends. Make them buy it. That's how you can do your part to make sure my daughter leads a comfortable life.

My family thanks you.

BIBLIOGRAPHY

Bean, Constance A. *Methods of Childbirth*. Dolphin Books, Doubleday & Company, Inc., 1972, 1982.

Curtis, Lindsay R., M.D., and Yvonne Coroles, R.N. *Pregnant and Loving It*. HP Books, 1977.

Danforth, David N. *The Complete Guide to Pregnancy*. Appleton-Century-Crofts, 1984.

Keith, Catherine. *The Birthing Book*. Times Books, 1984.

Lauersen, Niels H., M.D. *Childbirth with Love*. G.P. Putnam, 1983.

Lux Flanagan, Geraldine. *The First Nine Months of Life*. Touchstone Books, Simon and Schuster, 1962.

Rosengren Freedman, Helen. *Big Apple Baby*. Laurel-Howard, 1985.